Cooperstown

Cooperstown

By LOUIS C. JONES

with additional material by
WILLIAM J. GUILFOILE and
CLINTON VAN ZANDT HAWN, M.D.

New York State Historical Association
COOPERSTOWN, NEW YORK
1982

First edition copyright 1949 by the Otsego County Historical Society
Fourth edition revised copyright 1965 by the New York State Historical Association
Fifth edition revised 1982

Library of Congress Catalog Card Number 82-60416
ISBN: 0-917334-11-6
Printed in the United States of America
93 92 91 90 89 88 87 85 6 5 4 3 2

To the memory of
Stephen Carlton Clark, Sr.

Contents

Acknowledgements

IT IS now a third of a century since the first edition of this volume was published. A few anachronisms were corrected in the fourth edition in 1965 but not until now have we attempted to make any major changes. Mr. William Guilfoile of the National Baseball Hall of Fame and Museum has updated that chapter with an account of the radical changes in that popular institution. My old friend Clinton Van Zandt Hawn, M.D., for thirty-four years Chief Pathologist at the Mary Imogene Bassett Hospital, has written an entirely fresh history of the institution he served with such distinction. Our thanks also to Dr. Charles Ashley and Mr. Leon Bailey of the hospital staff. At the New York State Historical Association a number of staff have been invaluable: To Milo V. Stewart, Wendell Tripp, Ron Domin, Amelia Bielaski, Anne Bland, Beverly Olmsted, and Kathy Stocking I am indebted for a variety of crucial assistances. Finally, for encouragement and support I am grateful to my eminently successful successor, Minor Wine Thomas.

The Smithy, the first floor of which is the oldest structure in Cooperstown, built in 1786.

The Early Days

BETWEEN the surrender at Yorktown and the Treaty of Peace, General Washington took a little trip. He was tired and homesick, but until the British troops left New York for London, it might be just as well, thought Congress, if the General were within easy reach. There were scenes of action in the recent unpleasantness the General had missed and he set out to view them. From Lake George, he travelled up Lake Champlain to Crown Point; then to Schenectady, up the Mohawk Valley to Oneida Lake. He "traversed the country to the head of the eastern branch of the Susquehanna, and viewed the lake Otsego, and the portage between that Lake and the Mohawk River at Canajoharie."

There was a good reason for the visit of this first and most distinguished of the tourist wayfarers who came before the village of Cooperstown was even a dream in the hopeful minds of early settlers. The General was looking over the important scenes of his northern campaign; and, while no battle was fought in this place, a crucial victory was conceived and made possible here, one which he had helped plan.

In the early years of the Revolution, western New York (and that meant everything west of Schenectady) was an unprotected flank at the mercy of the Indian allies of the British and Loyalists. To eliminate this danger, in 1779, two American forces struck west into the wilderness against the Senecan strongholds in the Finger Lakes and Genesee Country. One of these forces, under General Sullivan, went west through Pennsylvania until it arrived eventually at Tioga Point on the Susquehanna River, where the men waited for the northern force under General Clinton.

General James Clinton gathered at Schenectady his share of the five thousand men Washington had thrown into his campaign. They marched along the Mohawk to Canajoharie and then turned south twenty miles to the head of Lake Otsego. It was a rough journey, those twenty miles, for the trail this army followed with its two hundred bateaux had to be made into a usable road. The shores of the lake were a wilderness that only a few white men had ever seen, but these soldiers had come on grim and sweaty business and scenery was not their seeking.

Nine miles the bateaux travelled down the lake, and at its foot they reached a little clearing and a log house or two belonging to a George Croghan, one whose name stands at the beginning of our local history but who is in Cooperstown little more than a name on musty deeds and mortgages. In this clearing the army camped while they cut great trees and dragged them to the spot where Lake Otsego gives birth to the Susquehanna River. During the summer they built a dam which raised the waters of the Otsego three or four feet. They built well, for sixty years later a few of the logs were still to be seen, but most of them had been knocked out on an August day in 1779 to carry a flood tide and two hundred soldier-filled boats down to Tioga Point and the awful destructive victories over the great chief Joseph Brant and his Iroquois braves.

Four years later, looking at the scene, Washington must have been impressed with the ingenuity of the scheme, and grateful to the men and leaders who made it a success. And visitors to Cooperstown still stand at the foot of River Street and gaze at the spot, marked with stone and bronze. Just off shore is Council Rock where the Indians used to gather, as every reader of *Deerslayer* so well knows, and there a few yards to the south was built the dam. It was more than a dam, of course, it was one of the stepping stones to our victory and our freedom.

* * *

There is a history of the village-site which no man will ever write; the story of the Indian settlers who had departed, for some reason of their own, before the white man came. They left notes for the historian, notes in arrow heads and stone implements beneath the surface, and apple trees which appear to have graced some early settlement, perhaps merely a summer colony; but when they came or why they left are secrets they took with them.

We cannot say, "Here was the red man's long house, here he had his fields," for we are not even positive this was true, but he has played his part in this town. Did not Cooper carry to the wide world scenes of Indians gathered here? Wherever English or the languages of Europe are read the doings of Chingachgook, Uncas and Hist are known. For a century and more these Indians have stood in the minds of millions as the very epitome of the Indian peoples.

Then too, there is the later story, told by the novelist's grandson, of that Indian buried in the customary sitting position underneath the stone wall which surrounds the Cooper grounds on River Street. This brave disapproved of walls, and winter after winter kicked this one down. Many men have wondered, with Robert Frost, about the "something there is that doesn't love a wall." There may be other answers over in New England, but in Cooperstown it's Indians.

When friends from out of town come here to visit, there is another Indian resting place they are shown. Nearly a century ago the bones of several Indians were found in Fernleigh-Over, the hillside east of the Susquehanna. These were buried together in a mound at the base of which, on a bronze plaque, are words composed by the Reverend William Wilberforce Lord, onetime rector in the village:

White Man, Greeting!

We, near whose bones you stand,
Were Iroquois. The wide land
Which now is yours was ours.
Friendly hands have given back
To us enough for a tomb.

* * *

In passing we have mentioned the name of George Croghan, the first major settler in the Otsego country of whom we have record. What we know of him concerns his tradings with the Indians and his vast dealings in thousands of acres of land rather than the man himself. His interest in the Otsego country was merely a passing incident in a long and ultimately disastrous career, but an incident in which were involved with him his friend, Sir William Johnson, and, as his fellow investor, Governor William Franklin, the illegitimate son of the great Ben, and later a Loyalist.

In 1769 and 1770 Croghan and ninety-nine shadowy partners acquired patents to a quarter of a million acres along Cherry Valley and Lake Otsego. He came to the foot of the lake in 1769 with carpenters, Irish bricklayers, masons, and Indian workers. They began a settlement: ten buildings were erected, four fields were cleared, a bridge was built across the Susquehanna, and a bateau was constructed. He had cattle, whose butter tasted of the wild garlic they fed upon in the

William Cooper. Oil on canvas by Gilbert Stuart, 1794.

Elizabeth Fenimore Cooper. Watercolor by George M. Freeman, 1816.

woods, and Johnson gave him fine sheep. Over the trail from the north came hogs, poultry, crockery, glass. Croghan's log house—there is a marker on Cooperstown's Main Street—was known well to travellers and Indians alike. His daughter, Susannah, and her husband, Lieutenant Augustine Prevost, came and settled at the head of the lake, and one might have guessed that the future of this valley lay in Croghan's hands. But Mr. Croghan, this ambitious Dubliner, had over-expanded and these acres were to slip between his fingers; he left behind him only his "hutt" and an emptied dream. Ironically, when General Clinton's troops quartered on his premises, they were preparing to wipe out the forces under the leadership of his other son-in-law, Joseph Brant, husband of Croghan's half-Indian daughter. By then Croghan, who cast his lot with the colonists, was far west in the Ohio country, breaking new ground.

If Croghan is a shadowy figure, William Cooper, who bought the Croghan tract at a sheriff's sale, stands etched in his own words and those of his articulate son. He once wrote down in good muscular prose the fruits of his pioneering experiences in a little volume called *A Guide in the Wilderness*; on those pages he can be seen in all his eighteenth century practicality. A simple, direct, capable, fair man—an aristocrat by instinct, but one suited to the fathering of democracy—his respect for the plain people and his rugged preference for them as neighbors and fellow workers in the task of beginning a new land are evident throughout his work.

In a time and in a state where the greatest landowners were thinking and acting as had the barons of the middle ages, Cooper stood out as a man fitted for the responsibilities of opening a frontier. His friends, the Hudson River landlords, were selling no land, but devising indentures which gave their tenants the shadow of independence but the reality of perpetual servitude. The sturdy judge sold his land outright, as much or as little as a man wished to buy, giving them seven to ten years in which to pay off the cost. Many of those who came were poor men, buying small, hundred-acre tracts. The testimony of Cooper's respect for these small holders and for the craftsmen who came to the village to contribute their skills is to be found on page after page of *A Guide in the Wilderness*. The result of this policy and this sensible, friendly attitude was that in the 1840s when the Hudson River counties were up in arms against their landlords, there was peace and order on the thousands of acres Cooper had settled.

William Cooper was a hard-headed dreamer, a highly civilized gentleman who made himself at one with the rough ways of the frontier, a stubborn man blessed with horse sense. History tells stories of him: In 1790, when his wife refused to leave the comfort of Burlington, New Jersey, for the wilderness, he had the chair from which she would not budge lifted onto a wagon and brought to Cooperstown, whether she would or no. Once he fought a political enemy on the village streets, and men were found afterward who took their solemn oaths that he was the winner. On a happier occasion he offered one hundred acres to any man who could throw him in a wrestling match and when, after several failed, he was finally beaten, he good-naturedly lived up to his bargain.

Cooper was politically an ardent Federalist and personally he governed his life on the principle that "physical and mental vigor alone would provide material wealth and grant the right to rule." Mistakenly, in 1799, he caused the arrest of Jedediah Peck, the man who is given credit for fathering the public school system of New York State, because Peck advocated the repeal of the Alien and Sedition Law. The sight of this beloved, one-eyed old man, carried in irons from Cooperstown to Albany, did much to bring about the Federalist defeat and the repeal of the law he hated. Cooper's friends were such Federalist stalwarts as Adams, Schuyler, Hamilton, Van Rensselaer, and when it was necessary to choose between Burr and Jefferson, he cast his vote for Burr. It was a period when violent party feeling was the order of the day, and one night in Albany in 1809, as he left a political meeting where he had spoken in a heated debate, he was felled by a blow on the head, struck by an unknown assailant from behind. Thus ended the man who had opened a wilderness in 1786 and lived to see it blossom into a valley of thriving farms with a bustling village at its heart.

* * *

Cooperstown began with a man's dream.

> In 1785, [wrote William Cooper long after] I visited the rough and hilly country of Otsego, where there existed not an inhabitant, nor any trace of a road; I was alone, three hundred miles from home, without bread, meat, or food of any

Presbyterian Church, the first in the village, 1805.

The Benjamin Griffin house, oldest residence in the village, built 1790.

kind; fire and fishing tackle were my only means of subsistence. I caught trout in the brook and roasted them on the ashes. My horse fed on the grass that grew by the edge of the waters. I laid me down to sleep in my watch coat, nothing but the melancholy wilderness around me. In this way, I explored the country, formed my plans of future settlement, and meditated upon the spot where a place of trade or a village should afterwards be established.

The next year, having bought part of the Croghan patent, Cooper opened 40,000 acres for sale and sixteen days later it was all taken up—mostly by "the poorest order of men." The years that followed were hard going:

But the greatest discouragement was in the extreme poverty of the people, none of whom had the means of clearing more than a small spot in the midst of the thick and lofty woods, so that their grain grew chiefly in the shade; their maize did not ripen, their wheat was blasted, and the little they did gather they had no mill to grind within twenty miles distance; not one in twenty had a horse, and the way lay through rapid streams, across swamps or over bogs. They had neither provisions to take with them nor money to purchase them; nor if

Pomeroy Place, William Cooper's wedding present to his daughter, Anne, and son-in-law, George Pomeroy. Detail, opposite page, shows the initials GAPC for George Ann Pomeroy Cooper and the date, 1804.

they had, were any to be found on their way. If the father of a family went abroad to labor for bread, it cost him three times its value before he could bring it home, and all the business on his farm stood still till his return.

I resided among them, and saw too clearly how bad this condition was. I erected a storehouse, and during each winter filled it with large quantities of grain, purchased in distant places. I procured from my friend Henry Drinker a credit for a large quantity of sugar kettles; he also lent me some potash kettles, which we conveyed as best we could, sometimes by partial roads or sleighs, and sometimes over the ice. By this means I established potash works among the settlers, and made them debtor for their bread and laboring utensils. I also gave them credit for their maple sugar and potash, at a price that would bear transportation, and the first year after the adoption of this plan, I collected in one mass forty-three hogsheads of sugar, and three hundred barrels of pot and pearl ash, worth about nine thousand dollars. This kept the people together and at home, and the country soon assumed a new face.

I had no funds of my own sufficient for the opening of new roads, but I collected the people at convenient seasons, and by joint efforts we were able to throw bridges over the deep streams, and to make, in the cheapest manner, such roads as suited our then humble purposes.

Judge Cooper gave his own name to the

village that had started with a few log houses left by Croghan. It was bounded by the lake on the north, the river on the east, Pioneer Street on the west. In the plans the Judge made in 1799 he foresaw the development going south toward what is now Beaver Street. The growth, however, wended toward the west, rather than south, so that the angular and rather meandering character of the streets in that part of town stems from the fact that no plan was made for them; Topsy-like, they grew.

One building stands from that earliest period. The smithy, on Pioneer Street between Main and Church, was built the first year of settlement, 1786. The two upper stories are a later addition, but the first floor, with its thick stone walls, so solidly built, was for many years the village blacksmith shop.

The first frame house was built by a widow named Johnson, but that, like its contemporaries, has vanished. It probably was not unlike the house built in 1790 for Benjamin Griffin which still stands at the northwest corner of Main and River Streets and is the oldest residence in town.

That was quite a year—1790—that, and the next. Judge Cooper brought his whole family from New Jersey to live in the frame house he had finished the year before. All told there were ten frame houses, three barns, and, after the Coopers and their servants had arrived in October, about half a hundred people. There was a store, a tannery, a smithy. But the next year, 1791, really saw the village fill out, so that the plans Judge Cooper had made three years earlier began to assume something of reality. Otsego County was formed and Cooperstown was named the county seat, with Cooper designated the first Judge of the County Court. Where Pioneer Street crosses Main a log and frame courthouse and jail was built; on the west side of Pioneer the long-to-be-renowned Red Lion Tavern was erected. It jutted into the middle of Main Street so that not until the terrible fire of 1862 could the street be of uniform width. Two lawyers came and several new stores opened; twenty homes were built—mostly by young couples with few children as yet. Two doctors came in 1791. "Doc" Powers was soon to be run out of town after he put an emetic in the rum punch at a party, but Doctor Fuller stayed on nearly half a century. Still another year was to pass before the first child was born and before a decision had to be made about where the burying ground would be.

Before William Cooper died in 1809 he saw many more changes, but no year like 1791. The first school came somewhere around 1793 and there was no clergyman to stay but for a night or two until 1795; for six months that year there was a Presbyterian preacher, but he went away and not until 1805 did the town have a church and that, too, was Presbyterian. It is the same church that still stands in the heart of the village, trim and high spired. It is a curious commentary on frontier life that there was a brewery in Cooperstown eleven years before there was a church.

Before the turn of the century there were mills, potteries, a tannery, a public library, roads and in 1795 a newspaper, owned by Elihu Phinney. The press on which it was printed was to grow to great fame, for Phinney's almanacs and Bibles were to become household commonplaces in all the homes of western York State.

And along with the buildings and population was growing an intense local pride, a sure knowledge that this was the fairest village that ever had been or ever would be. Thus, when the court sought a terrible punishment for the evil doer, something far more salutory than the jail or stocks, it decreed banishment, for surely nothing could be worse than never again to be permitted to see a winter sunrise over Mount Vision or a spring sunset reflected on the tree covered flanks of the Sleeping Lion. The viewpoint still prevails.

The Novelist and His Times

AS THE village was growing up, so with it grew the youngest son of Judge Cooper, James, later James Fenimore. At first, with his four brothers and two sisters, he lived in the frame house his father had built to receive his family in 1790. Nine years later they all moved into Otsego Hall, the noblest mansion west of Albany, with a prospect which included the whole length of Lake Otsego. The building, which burned in 1853, stood where Victor Salvatore's statue of the novelist now dominates the park appropriately known as the Cooper Grounds.

This is not the place to evaluate the work of Cooper the novelist but perhaps the reader should be reminded of his indisputable contribution to American letters. He was the first novelist to depict on a grand scale the American wilderness and the civilization of our frontier; he created, in Leatherstocking, our first great fictional character, one who was not only an individual but a symbol of an important type in our national history, the rootless forerunner of the first settlers. It is easy enough to criticize Cooper's tortuous style, his unrealistic conversations, his fatuous "females," his endless descriptions, but he remains one of our literary giants and as much a pioneer in our literature as his father was in the wilderness. More than any other writer until the advent of Mark Twain, Cooper gave Europeans their most convincing picture of our country.

Two of his five books about Leatherstocking have the Otsego country for their setting. *The Deerslayer* (1841) depicts the lake before white civilization had touched it and when Council Rock was an Indian meeting point. Deerslayer, (*alias* Leatherstocking, *alias* Hawkeye, *alias* Natty Bumppo, *alias* Pathfinder) is here a young white man, raised by the Delawares, thus a product of both white and Indian civilizations. The book has given us such place names in and about the Lake as Point Judith, Natty Bumppo's cave, Hutter's Castle, Leatherstocking Falls, and there are scenes in the book located all along the western shore and the outlet to the Susquehanna River.

While *The Deerslayer* was the last of the Leatherstocking books to be written and the first in the chronology of the hero's life, *The Pioneers* (1823) was the first of the series that Cooper wrote. The setting is Cooperstown as it was in his own boyhood, and Judge Templeton is a slightly disguised Judge Cooper. This creative work and a short history of the community which Cooper wrote in 1838, *The Chronicles of Cooperstown*, are among the best sources we have of the early days in the village.

Because James Fenimore Cooper carried the name of this place to the far corners of the world and because he played an important, if sometimes unhappy, part in its history, he must loom large in even the briefest account of Cooperstown.

He was a year old when he arrived here with his mother and brothers and sisters in 1790 to inhabit the frame house his father had readied for their coming. As a growing boy he roamed the woods and fished the Lake for the Otsego bass which still draw fishermen from miles around. In 1799 the family moved into Otsego Hall, then characterized by simplicity and grandeur. When James was ten he went to Albany to prepare for Yale, which he entered at thirteen. He stayed at Yale for three years;

Otsego Hall, a photograph showing the Gothic elements that the novelist added, ca. 1852.

in his junior year he was dismissed for the infraction of one of those rules which were intended to keep undergraduates of his time in line. So it was that he came back to Otsego Hall for two months in 1806 before he was articled to Captain Johnson of the merchantman *Sterling* and went to sea. From his experiences during years immediately following came the first American novels of life before the mast, at a time when our merchant fleet was gaining a position of eminence in the sea lanes of the world.

In 1811 Cooper left the Navy, to which he had been transferred, and soon after married Susan Augusta DeLancey of the Loyalist landholding Westchester family; for a few years he fitted into the world of his wife's family, but the call of the hills could not be denied and he and his young family came back to Cooperstown. His mother, widowed since 1809, was living in Otsego Hall, so that his first move was the construction of a small frame house on Fenimore Farm to serve as a stop-gap until his larger plans for a suitable stone dwelling could be completed. Those were happy days; he was active in the community and busy with projects which would have made him a typical country gentleman. Two children were born here and one was buried across the little brook which runs by

James Fenimore Cooper. Oil on canvas by John Wesley Jarvis, ca. 1820.

the present Fenimore House. Then, in 1817, the family moved back to Westchester, not to return again for seventeen years.

When he did come back it was after the literary acclaim of two continents and years of living in Europe where he had known the great figures of his time and been recognized as one of them. He returned to an America greatly changed from the land he had left, and to a Cooperstown that did not know him. Although he had been one of America's most consistent defenders in Europe, there was much of the aristocrat in his social philosophy. Unfortunately his high regard for the rights of property soon involved him in an unhappy quarrel with the local community. A

Leatherstocking Meets the Law, *by John Quidor, 1832. A scene from Cooper's* The Pioneers.

The Turkey Shoot, *by Tompkins Matteson, 1857. A scene from* The Pioneers.

mountain grew out of a mole hill. It began when Cooper forbade the village folk from using Three Mile Point, which he owned but which had been used as a community picnic ground since his father's day without let or hindrance. Bitter reports, then diatribes in the press, then a long series of libel suits wrote a discordant chapter into village history. When it was all over Cooper had been justified in the courts, but he had few friends left in his old home. Wise or foolish in pressing the case against his neighbors and their metropolitan editorial defenders, Cooper, as Robert Spiller has said, "established the right of the individual in a democracy to certain immunities. His character could not be publicly attacked without evidence of the truth of the charges. Upon this basis of individual immunity, a social structure which recognized differences in the individuals which compose it, could be built. American democracy today takes such differences for granted, in its social if not its political composition. In Cooper's day it did not." Thus a quarrel which began with Cooper's concern for his property rights ended with a legal clarification of the personal rights of each of us. The battle over Three Mile Point wrote into law the basic decisions in matters of libel.

The novelist's last years in Cooperstown were lonely; when he walked along the streets the friendly greetings were few enough, although a little girl who lived nearby remembered him as one who had time for her and gallant courtesy for the wife he had long loved. He died in 1851 and two years later Otsego Hall, with the Gothic crenelations he had added to give it an old-world look, burned to the ground.

* * *

The catalog of famous men whose lives became intertwined with the history of this village is remarkable for a community that has seldom numbered more than 2500 inhabitants. Many of the illustrious ones were not natives, but people who turned to the quiet of the place as to a refuge away from the hurly-burly of their careers. These were the glittering lights who carried the name of the town far afield, but the town they were proud of was not created by them. It was the unconscious product of the people whose names do not loom large in the histories; the decent, honest merchants, the fine carpenters who knew how to build a house to please the eye and last the centuries, the tanners and coopers who could turn out a soft piece of leather or a snug tub, the printers who could set the type for Bibles and broadsides, the farm people from the neighboring hills. These men and their wives created an atmosphere of peace and dignity to which more famous folk could come for respite from a tumultuous world.

Judge Samuel Nelson was one of those who came to strike roots in Cooperstown, one who added to her renown and one whom generations were proud to honor. For fifty years he dignified the bench, in the Sixth Circuit, on the Supreme Court of the State, on the United States Supreme Court from 1845 to 1872.

On two great occasions Nelson was the center of dramatic events in Cooperstown. Once, during the Civil War, Secretary of State Seward brought the entire diplomatic corps to the village on a tour of the industrial North designed to impress the representatives of foreign powers with the Federal war potential. Possibly the real reason for bringing this distinguished company to non-industrial Cooperstown in the August of 1863 was the fact that President Lincoln and Secretary Seward were anxious to have an unofficial and unpublicized opinion from Justice Nelson, a Democrat, on the constitutionality of the Draft Law. A midnight meeting of the Secretary and Justice took place after the various plenipotentiaries had been bedded down in the best homes in town. Before dawn Seward was in a position to assure his President that Nelson considered the law constitutional.

Ten years later when the Judge retired from the bench there was another great day—a winter day—when the flag flew and men of legal renown from the great world outside came to honor the handsome, beloved old man. When he died a few months later one of the noble spirits who was loved along the streets and country roads was gone—not a shaker of dynasties but one of the builders of an orderly society.

An earlier figure than Nelson, but equally important in his own way, was Elihu Phinney, who opened his printing press and started a newspaper in 1795. The Phinney Almanac was, next to the Bible which he also printed in amazing numbers, the most important reading matter on the New York frontier. Farmers read it with reverence in planning their farm work, turned to it for information agricultural, astronomical, astrological. York State farmers used to tell of the year when Phinney's Almanac, through a printer's error, predicted snow on July 4. Lo and behold! July 4th came and snow with it. No copy of

James Fenimore Cooper's library, from a drawing by G. Pomeroy Keese.

that issue has ever been found, but the story is a clue to Phinney's standing in the countryside. In 1838 the firm of H. & H.E. Phinney employed forty workers to print 8000 Bibles, 60,000 books—mostly school texts—and 200,000 almanacs. It was the Phinneys' brag that they printed the biggest and smallest Bibles in existence and they may well have been correct. Certainly they were pioneers in book merchandising, for out from Cooperstown they sent wagons fitted as traveling bookstores, carrying their books to the farms and villages where literature was a rarity and any book welcome. Keeping up with the times, after the Erie Canal was dug, Phinney had floating bookstores from Albany to Buffalo. And the printing house of Phinney was one of the important factors in giving Cooperstown its early reputation as a centre of culture. One of the homes built by the Phinney family now houses the Cooper Inn on Chestnut Street.

Thurlow Weed, the master politician of the middle of the century, spent a few eventful months in Cooperstown, months which must have been called to mind repeatedly through-

Dedication of Cooper's statue in Cooperstown, 1940. Dixon Ryan Fox, Owen D. Young, Stephen C. Clark, Sr., James Fenimore Cooper IV, and the sculptor, Victor Salvatore.

out his life. He tells the story in his autobiography:

In April 1814, after the election, I packed my movables in a handkerchief, and started on foot for Cooperstown, where I obtained work in the office of H. & E. Phinney. Cooperstown was then a bright, active, growing, and pleasant village. I boarded with Mrs. Ostrander, to whose daughter I became attached; but as I was only in my seventeenth year, and of unsettled and uncertain habits, and the young lady in her sixteenth year, her friends deemed it their duty to interpose, which they did strenuously. I did not think this unreasonable, having a distrust of my fitness for such responsibility. We agreed therefore to separate, with the understanding that if, after the lapse of three or four years, our affection remained unaltered, the engagement should be renewed.

During my residence in Cooperstown an incident occurred which, as it obtained considerable notoriety many years afterwards, requires notice here. In the company of four young men I attended a Sunday evening Methodist meeting, where, during the service, our attention was attracted to a group of girls who were by no means seriously impressed. At the close of the meeting we joined them and accompanied them to the tavern, where a conveyance awaited the party, as they resided several miles out of the village. The following day a man appeared in the village to identify the young men, who, as he alleged, had committed a gross misdemeanor. And at the next session of the grand jury these young men including myself, were indicted. The other young men, being natives of the village were reputably connected, readily obtained bail, while I, being a stranger, felt delicate about asking such a favor. While thus painfully embarrassed, my bond was unexpectedly signed by Israel W. Clark, editor of the "Watch Tower," and Ambrose L. Jordan, then a young lawyer recently from Columbia, his native county, became my volunteer counsel. Many years afterwards I was informed by those gentlemen that they were prompted by the young lady to whom I have referred, and who requested them not to let me know to whose kind offices I was indebted for bondsman and counsel. Messrs. Clark and Jordan became my warm friends, and remained so to the end of their long and useful lives. It was my privilege and pleasure in after life to reciprocate the services they rendered me at a trying moment.

Early in February it became necessary for Weed to reappear at Cooperstown. The trial, having been put over from the October term in consequence of his absence in the army, came on immediately and, as history has been recorded, the jury acquitted him without leaving their seats. It is pleasant to remember that in time Weed and his loyal "young lady friend" were happily married—giving the incident its suitable close.

A youthful contemporary of Weed's was

William L. Stone, who was apprenticed to Colonel Prentiss, editor of the *Cooperstown Federalist*, and who was in later life to become the nationally known editor of *The Commercial Advertiser* of New York, and the biographer of both Red Jacket and Joseph Brant. As a young man who had walked to Cooperstown for his first job, he had been a friend of James Fenimore Cooper, but from 1840 to 1844, he was involved in a series of libel suits against Cooper which began with an unfavorable book review and ended after Stone's death.

The written word has played a striking part in the village's history. Not only have six generations of the Cooper family enriched our literature, but there have also been the legal decisions of Nelson, the legal orations of its distinguished barristers, the Bibles, newspapers and almanacs of Phinney, and the not inconsiderable nor unimportant literary publications of Erastus "Dime Novel" Beadle (1821–1894) whose books were as exciting to boys and as annoying to parents as were the comic books of a later day. Hidden underneath mattresses and the rafters of haylofts, they all had the qualities which the "proper" juvenile books of his time lacked: action, ex-

Graves of James Fenimore Cooper and his wife in Christ Church graveyard.

Judge Samuel Nelson. Oil on canvas by Carl Brandt, 1864.

citing pictures, conversations somewhat closer to reality than was the mode.

Beadle had learned to handle type in the print shop of the Phinneys, and had gone on to Buffalo to publish a magazine called *Youth's Casket*, then to New York to publish ten cent, pocket-sized song books, joke books, biographies, recitations and other descendants of the early chapbooks. Beadle never wrote the novels associated with his name, but the novels he soon began to publish followed a rigid pattern he established: Virtue was always rewarded; sin was punished; morality triumphed. The trouble was that virtue was so breathlessly exciting in coming to its triumph that Victorian parents who suspected that nothing could be both moral and fun, considered the Dime Novels of Mr. Beadle a dangerous influence. They were trash, but they seem like innocuous trash to us, and the wonder of them is the noise they made in the world.

The modern Cooperstown as we see it today, is largely, except for scores of private residences, a post-Civil War development. One reason for this was the fire of April 10, 1862, that began along Main Street and wiped out a third of the business section. One result of this catastrophe was that Main Street could become of uniform width, for from earliest times that part west of Pioneer had been narrower than the older, more easterly section. The buildings that rose above the ashes were built in the manner fashionable in the 1860s. The names of the store fronts change, the interiors are modernized, new signs put in an appearance, but the basic pattern changes but little. There is general acceptance of the zoning laws which keep it that way.

The changes throughout the village after the fire were so gradual and so in tune with what was happening elsewhere that they caused hardly a ripple. The water works expanded, a gas company came on the scene, the telephone began as a local service but shortly was connected to other towns. The trolley connecting Oneonta with Mohawk came, flourished and died. Autos and movies brought the outside world to us and took us to the outside world but certain basic patterns of the whole community give evidence of immutability. The Indians, apparently, came to their settlement at the headwaters of the Susquehanna only in the summer. Their settlement was not one for the year round but a place for the warm months only. And James Fenimore Cooper, writing of the village in 1838, has a most interesting passage which carries insight both to the history of the community as a summer resort and to the mind and viewpoint of that aristocratic democrat:

> We shall have no mushroom city, but there is little doubt that in the course of time, as the population of the country fills up, this spot will contain a provincial town of importance. The beauty of its situation, the lake, the purity of the air, and the other advantages pointed out, seem destined to make it more peculiarly a place of resort, for those who live less for active life than for its elegance and ease. It is highly probable that, half a century hence, the shores of the lake will be lined with country residences, when the village will be the center of their supplies of every kind. Were an effort made, even now, by the erection of proper lodging houses, the establishment of reading rooms and libraries, and the embellishment of a few of the favorable spots, in the way of public promenades and walks, it strikes us that it would be quite easy to bring the place into request, as one of resort for the inhabitants of the large towns during the warm months.

To a certain extent the last century brought into being Cooper's elegant vision. Cooperstown and the shores of Lake Otsego became the summer residence for scores of well-to-do families who opened their fine houses in June and lingered only until the first frosts. The village, as they remembered its vernal warmth

The north side of Main Street at Pioneer before the fire of 1862. Below: A view of Main Street, after the fire, looking north. The Cooper Inn, partly obscured, can be seen in the center.

and the gaiety of the summer social life, must have meant much to many of them. But few of them were ever a part of the village. To belong, really to be of the village—and it is safe to say this has long been true—one must walk along Main Street when the snow is a mountain range between walk and road, when neighbors talk of thirty and forty below zero, when one listens to the old timers admit that this winter is the worst they remember.

The great change in Cooperstown in recent years has been wrought by the fact that it has been discovered and rediscovered by thousands of families of modest means bent on filling a brief vacation with memorable experiences. There has taken place, then, a kind of democratization of summertime Cooperstown. Yet despite this change the village has kept its historic spirit and its gracious dignity, primarily because it is those who make their homes here the year round that give the place its character. In recent years the hospital and the educational institutions in the village have brought in an increasing number of families who have been happy to fit into this spirit, and to contribute to it and strengthen it.

Kingfisher Tower

Lake Otsego

THE INDIANS are said to have called it "O-te-sa-ga" and Cooper called it "The Glimmerglass" but call it what you will the Lake dominates the town and the area, not only for the nine miles north in which it lies, but for a considerable distance back on either shore.

Everyone who writes about it grows lyrical. Some of Cooper's best prose is his description of it as Leatherstocking first saw it; all of the historians who have written of this place have done their best to capture in words some of the charm the Lake exerted over them. We would mention only its infinite variety—the purple shadows of a summer sunset, the white gleam on the ice when the snow covers its length and the fishermen's shanties form curious little villages on its face, and those glorious moments in the summer when, with the water blue as azure and the sun bright in the sky, the white sails of the fleet go skimming back and forth along its length, up, around the buoy and down again toward the finish line.

For nine miles Otsego stretches almost north and south and the hills pile up on either side. Those to the east are almost entirely wooded, those to the west show great patches of tillable land dotted with orchards. At the head is "The Sleeping Lion," which seems to brood over the upper reaches. At the foot of the Lake lies the village itself.

Few lakes in America in so small a compass have gathered in so much romance, legend, and history. Not to write of the Lake in writing of Cooperstown would be like writing of Springfield, Illinois and not mentioning Lincoln. Otsego is our most distinguished citizen.

Spring comes slowly in the Otsego hills. One of the signs of its coming is to be seen along Main Street as people put their money down on the ice pool. All the old timers and all the youngsters just learning the ropes and the newcomers who like to take a gamble for a gamble's sake each choose a date on which the ice will be out of the Lake. Financially speaking, the operation is insignificant; in terms of the seasonal movements of the town it is of considerable importance. And after the ice is out of the Lake, the boats come out of winter storage. Down at the foot of Fair Street, just to the west of the outlet where the Susquehanna begins its long meander to the sea, the boats are brought from winter hiding, and the owners tune up the motors or patch their sails, do a little caulking here and a little painting there, take them out for a trial run, drop down a line to see how the fishing's going to be this year. All through the months until November the foot of Fair Street will be the very core of life for many a lover of the Lake. Here, too, the tourists and summer visitors go to take the ride around the Lake in the motor launch. There have been tourist boats of various kinds and descriptions for generations. There was the "Natty Bumppo" that Abiather Watkins made famous in these parts, there were others before and others since, and today happily again one can make the grand tour of the Lake. It has been traditional with writers about this area that they take their readers on such a voyage and this temptation we cannot resist.

As the boat swings out into the Lake, one would do well to look back toward the point where the Susquehanna forms the outlet of the Lake. There are two boulders, one marking Clinton's Dam, of which we have spoken

Council Rock

before, and another which has long been known as Council Rock. There is considerable evidence, not only in Cooper's books but elsewhere, that Council Rock was an actual meeting place for the Indians.

The old Mohawk Indians say that once, long before the white man was a frequenter of the Lake, one of the black-robed missionaries came to the Indian settlement. He preached to them of his God and his religion and he spoke disparagingly of their own faith. They listened to him patiently, especially when he spoke of the great power of his God. His God, he said, could move mountains, could perform, indeed, any miracle man could conceive. Finally one of the chiefs of the village looked at him and asked "Have you faith in this God of yours?" and the missionary replied with certainty that he had. "Have you faith that this God of yours can move mountains?" And the missionary again was emphatic. Then said the chief, "Do you have faith that your God can move the rock that stands there," pointing to Council Rock, and again with the utmost emphasis the missionary insisted that he could. "Well, then" said the chief, "we will test your faith. We will roll the rock on top of you and your faith being what it is, your God will move it off your back." The rock was rolled on top of him and the Indians waited for his faith to manifest itself and for his God to act for him. And if you listen to the Mohawks there is still under the rock the skeleton of that man of great faith.

As you look up from the rock, two handsome homes will catch your eye. One is Lakelands, built in 1804 by John Myer Bowers, whose father Henry Bowers had acquired the property in 1791. Lakelands stands today almost exactly as it was built. During the 19th century it was "modernized" with a mansard roof and other embellishments, but in 1946 it was restored to its pristine charm. One of the most interesting occupants of that or any house in the village was probably John Myer Bowers' mother-in-law, Mrs. Martha Stewart, whose father and husband had both been on Washington's staff and who was close to the Washington family not only during the Revolution but in the later years of the first presidency. Her memories of that period of which she was an intimate observer were listened to with delight in Cooperstown for nearly half a century. It was her daughter, Mrs. Bowers, who remembered sitting, as a child of three, on Washington's knee while he sang a nonsense verse to her:

There was an old, old man and an old, old
  woman
They lived in a vinegar bottle together
Shelter'd alike from wind and from weather
They lived in a vinegar bottle together.

Farther up on the foot of Mount Vision stands a stone neoclassic house built in 1829 by Judge Eben Morehouse. It was the scene of one of our local anecdotes. It concerns the occasion in 1839 when Judge Morehouse was the host to Martin Van Buren, then President of the United States. It was a good party at which no man could deprecate his host's hospitality. Nor was Martin Van Buren one to neglect the flowing bowl. After the other guests were out of the way the guest of honor and an intimate who had come with him began their journey back to their lodgings. Some will tell you they were on horseback, some will say they were on foot, but whichever the case, the gentlemen became lost and for hours wandered about the estate looking for the gatehouse and the road back to town. In the morning the gardens were found to have been trampled and broken during their befuddled wanderings. Cooperstown can still chuckle over a distinguished guest whose capacities were not up to Cooperstown hospitality.

The boat is now moving up the east shore of the Lake opposite Fairy Springs Park where village people picnic and go swimming. Everyone is looking ahead to Point Judith, and Kingfisher Tower. Back in the hills is Natty Bumppo's Cave which provided Elizabeth Temple with a refuge from the forest fire in Cooper's novel, *The Pioneers*, and which was the scene of Captain Hollister's charge at the head of Templeton's Light Infantry in the same novel. It should be observed that Cooper deliberately made the cave larger in the novel than it is in actuality. On the Lake, opposite the cave is the best echo and it is here that the old Black, Joe Tom, when he was taking parties around the Lake always called out, "Natty Bumppo! Natty Bumppo!" and Natty Bumppo's echo would come rolling back from the hillside above.

Kingfisher Tower is a typical example of nineteenth-century romanticism as it frequently exhibited itself in America. It was erected by Edward Clark in 1876 at a time when many in the community were out of employment and, undoubtedly, one of the purposes in building it was to provide work. The tower was criticized then as it has been criticized since and some called it "Clark's Folly" but at the request of the local paper Clark wrote an account of it which he published anonymously:

Kingfisher Tower consists of a miniature castle, after the style of the eleventh and twelfth centuries, standing upon the extremity of the Point and rising out of the water to a height of nearly

Lakelands as it is today. Opposite page, as it looked with Victorian "modernization," and as it looked originally.

sixty feet. It forms an objective point in the scene presented by the Lake and surrounding hills; it adds solemnity to the landscape, seeming to stand guard over the vicinity, while it gives a character of antiquity to the Lake, a charm by which we cannot help being impressed in such scenes. The effect of the structure is that of a picture from medieval times, and its value to the lake is very great. Mr. Clark has been led to erect it simply by desire to beautify the lake and add an attraction which must be seen by all who traverse the lake or drive along its shores. They whose minds can rise above simple notions of utility to an appreciation of art joined to nature, will thank him for it.

The explanation is as much a period piece as the building.

From Point Judith for some miles north the forest comes down to the very edge of the Lake, the banks are precipitous in this section on the east shore and so, despite the occasional summer camp hidden in the trees, it must have very much the same look that it had in the days of Clinton's expedition. Seven miles up, the Lake widens as Hyde Bay cuts into the eastern shore. For many decades the oldest and shortest covered bridge in New York spanned Shadow Brook just north of its entrance to the Lake. The bridge has now been moved closer to Hyde Hall which it has always served.

At the head of Hyde Bay, lying at the foot of Mount Wellington, known as the Sleeping Lion, is Glimmerglass State Park. On a slight rise above the beach and the campground stands Hyde Hall, a handsome example of Georgian architecture. The main part of the building was built in 1815 for George Clarke and then eighteen years later additions were made with the advice of Philip Hooker, one of the great architects of the Nationalist period. The vast land holdings of the Clarke family went back to the mid-eighteenth cen-

Hyde Hall

tury when one of their ancestors, another George Clarke, was a lieutenant governor of the Colony of New York. The traditions of this house are the traditions of the English landed gentry and it claims more than its fair share of the romance and folklore of the region.

Ralph Birdsall, that excellent teller of *The Story of Cooperstown*, has a passage which well illustrates some of the reasons why this is so:

In his habits and sentiments Clarke was thoroughly English. He delighted to have his dinner got up in old English style, with the best of roast beef and mutton, garnished with such delicacies as the lake and country afforded, and just such as his countrymen, who knew how to appreciate good things, would order, were they the caterers; and in these particulars he hardly ever failed to excel. Not only were his household arrangements in this style, but he was English in his religious views; unless these matters were held in conformity to the Anglican Church they were not acceptable.

When Clarke's son George, who afterwards succeeded to the estate, was baptized, in 1824, Father Nash officiated, and several other clergymen of the Episcopal Church were in attendance, besides some guests from Utica, and many from Cooperstown and the surrounding country who had come to Hyde Hall for the occasion. The christening was performed with suitable gravity, and in due time the dinner was announced, which was in the substantial excellent style that Clarke knew well how to order for such a festivity. The host was talkative and charming; as the dinner proceeded the guests became increasingly good-humored, exceedingly well satisfied with him and with themselves. "In due time the ladies and clergy retired," says Levi Beardsley, who was present at the feast, "and then the guests were effectually plied with creature comforts."

Nothing seemed more delightful to the first proprietor of Hyde Hall than thus to sit in company with congenial men at the flowing bowl; to begin in the enjoyment of rational conversation; to discuss literature and art and statecraft; to warm up to the telling of rare stories and the singing of good songs; and, in the end, to get his guests, or a portion of them, "under the table." On this occasion, after partaking of the viands and good cheer, the guests left the table in the early part of the evening, and repaired to the plateau in front of the house, where some of them ran foot-races in the dark, with no great credit to themselves as pedestrians. As they were going back into the house, one of the guests stumbled and fell into the hall, where he lay for some time, obstructing the closing of the outer door. One of the servants came to Clarke, who had retired for the night, and asked what he should do with the large gentleman who had fallen in the doorway, and was unable to rise. "Drag him in, and put him under the table" was the order which was immediately complied with, and under the table the fallen guest remained until morning.

Comparatively speaking, the east shore of the Lake is uninhabited. The whole west shore is dotted with summer cottages and an occasional estate of size and grandeur. As early as 1762 one Nicholas Lowe of New York had built a mill there and by 1769 George Croghan's son-in-law, Captain Augustine Prevost, had cleared sixteen or eighteen acres, built a log house and erected a new sawmill on the site. There is an active tradition that the present attractive house includes that original log house, disguised under plaster and paint. Be that as it may, the property at Swanswick

The covered bridge spanning Shadow Brook.

Swanswick, above, and close-up of the Swanswick weathervane, opposite page.

has probably been occupied by white men longer than any other on the Lake. James Fenimore Cooper, grandson of the novelist, in his charming little pamphlet, *Reminiscences of Mid-Victorian Cooperstown*, quotes a letter written by Prevost in which he says that all of his children were suffering from "the hooping cough" which he found annoying, as well might the father of twenty-one children.

For three miles south of Swanswick the west shore is well lined with small summer camps. One comes to Hutter's Point where Deerslayer first saw the Lake. According to Cooper's novel, the Sunken Islands on which Hutter had built his curious house on stilts were located near Hutter's Point. Actually, the Sunken Islands are a little farther north, and just as he changed the actual facts about Natty Bumppo's cave to meet his literary need so he moved the Sunken Islands farther down the Lake. The whole middle section of the Lake is of special interest to those familiar with *The Deerslayer*, for much of the action takes place between Hutter's Point and Three Mile Point. The southern end of the Lake is more particularly of interest to those familiar with *The Pioneers*.

Hickory Grove, Five Mile Point and Three Mile Point have been famous in their day for their inns, but of these only Hickory Grove, about a mile above Five Mile Point, still survives. Excepting Cooperstown itself Three Mile Point is more richly endowed with tradition than any other location on the Lake. Here are some of the most famous scenes in

The Deerslayer; it was here that Chingachgook kept his tryst with Wah-ta-wah and with the help of Deerslayer escaped from the Hurons. Three Mile Point has been, since the earliest times of the Cooper occupancy, a picnic ground and a place of pleasure. The wild roses which grew along the hillside caused it to be known, before its more prosaic name was given it, as "Wild Rose Point." We have already spoken of the significance of this little jut of land in our legal history and in the biography of Cooper. Today the Point is still a rendezvous for summer outings and a place where any resident of Cooperstown may go with his friends to picnic or swim. In the winter time, out on the Lake stands the biggest colony of fishing shanties just opposite the Point.

On the western hillside above Three Mile Point stand the houses of August Busch, the St. Louis brewer who bought the land when it

Natty Bumppo's cave in the hills on the eastern shore of the lake.

Natty Bumppo II on the Glimmerglass.

produced some of the finest local hops, so sought after by brewers everywhere. Mr. Busch had a great sense of the dramatic and a sense of fun. He kept an elephant pastured on his front lawn and in 1934, when the Singer Midgets came to town, he entertained them all.

A mile south along the shore stands Brookwood which was a house of mystery in the youth of James Fenimore Cooper, grandson of the novelist and author of *Mid-Victorian Cooperstown.* The story he tells goes back to the early 1850's when

> an English gentleman giving the name of Captain Daniels arrived in Cooperstown. He bought Brookwood and furnished it completely, left town and soon returned with a very beautiful woman whom he introduced as his wife. Here they lived for some time, keeping much to themselves. One day they were gone. Who they were and where they went no one ever knew. All the contents of the house were sold at auction and my grandmother bought and gave to my mother when she was married a very beautiful and unusual silver teapot marked with a much-worn coat of arms, which still is in the family.

Along the shore below Brookwood are the rolling hills of Fenimore Farm and eventually Fenimore House, headquarters of the New York State Historical Association, and its adjacent library. This is the site of the home of James Fenimore Cooper and later of Judge Samuel Nelson. Next to Fenimore House is

The Singer Midgets on stage at Smalley's Theater in Cooperstown.

Three Mile Point. Oil on canvas by Louis R. Mignot and Julius Gollman, showing leading citizens of the 1850s.

the golf course and the club house and the little bay once known as "Rat's Cove" and later, in a more romantic period, as "Blackbird Bay." From this point on the Lake and from Brookwood begin the sailboat regattas, the loveliest sight of the summertime.

Now we are back opposite Cooperstown itself, and the great building which dominates that end of the Lake is the Hotel Otesaga. The land where the building stands was once known as "the Hausman lot," and there potters found a fine pink clay.

Esaias Hausman was a quiet character who came to the village in 1801 and bought land from Judge Cooper. He appeared, neatly dressed but barefoot, garbed in the clothing typical of a sailor. When he asked Judge Cooper how much the land would cost and the judge told him, he took out a bag of gold coins which hung around his neck and paid the price without any question. He built himself a little rough house and lived there for years. He was well educated, spoke several languages, seemed to be conversant with the classics; he taught Hebrew to the president of one of the nearby colleges. Sometimes he was away for months and when he was in Cooperstown he had little to do with his neighbors. There were stories that he had fought in Napoleon's army, that he had narrowly escaped the guillotine. What his history was, no man knew, but when he died in 1812 they found still between his shoulder blades a bag of gold coins.

Rounding the buoy, summer regatta on Lake Otsego.

During the time it has taken us to tell Hausman's little tale the boat has brought us back to the dock and the tour of the Lake is over. But before we leave the dock it is always worthwhile to take one long look up to the Sleeping Lion, for never for two moments in succession are the lights the same upon this romantic Lake and despite all its mystery and romance and its history, its greatest charm remains, as we said when we began, in its infinite variety as the sunlight and the moonlight strike it from ever-changing angles.

The Modern Village

IT COULD be argued that Cooperstown has had a special kind of luck which has eventually turned its apparent liabilities into assets. In the nineteenth century, first the canal, then the railroad, passed it by, but what at the time seemed tragedies made it possible for the village to retain in a later more hectic age a quality of Victorian repose. The winters were always harsh and the snow discouragingly frequent—a fact of local life which, in the age of ski enthusiasts and ice fishing, is no great disadvantage. In the second half of the nineteenth century a single family came to control a very large portion of the village and surrounding lands and this might easily have eventually stultified the community; but members of the family in question were blessed with a sure sense of civic responsibility, so that many of the institutions which today set the village apart have stemmed from their imaginative leadership. Moreover, in recent years the Clark family has been steadily transferring a large part of its holdings to philanthropic and educational institutions.

Edward Clark came to Cooperstown in the period immediately before the Civil War; his wife, the daughter of his law partner, Ambrose L. Jordan, had been born here. Jordan, the son of a Connecticut farmer who had fought in the Revolution, had grown up near Hudson, Columbia County, but came to Cooperstown in 1813, at the outset of his legal career. He was an ardent Democrat and the political heir of Jedediah Peck, Judge Cooper's old enemy. Historians speak of Jordan as a handsome, eloquent man, with a soft voice and a tongue capable of the bitterest vituperation—so bitter that he was called "Aqua Fortis" Jordan by his fellow attorneys. During his years in Cooperstown, 1813 to 1820, he was a leading political and legal figure.

He returned to Hudson in 1820 where he stood up against Elisha Williams, "the undisputed colossus of the courts." In the long, drawn out legal battles of the Antirent Wars he was frequently attorney for the Down Rent farmers and the opponent of the feudal landowners. With these predilections in mind, the people chose him to serve on the New York Constitutional Convention of 1846 and later as Attorney General of the State. This convention wrote finis to the system of land tenure which had made the great Hudson River families so powerful and which had aroused the fighting anger of the farmers.

In the meantime Jordan had taken into his law office as clerk a young Williams College graduate from Athens, Greene County, named Edward Clark, son of Nathan Clark, a leading potter of the Hudson Valley. This was in 1830; five years later the young man married Jordan's daughter, Caroline, who had been born in Cooperstown, and in 1837 the law firm of Jordan & Clark was formed.

It is interesting to note that Jordan, who had no love for James Fenimore Cooper, successfully defended James Watson Webb, editor of the *New York Courier and Enquirer*, when the novelist sued Webb in one of his many libel suits. During the trial Jordan read the entirety of Cooper's *Home as Found* to the jury, with caustic observations on the author interspersed.

About 1848 Isaac M. Singer came to the firm of Jordan & Clark, by that time in New York City, for help in clearing the title to a wood carving machine he had invented. From this first contact came Clark's growing association with Singer, who was soon to make a sewing machine of practical use. Clark became Singer's partner and the business head of the partnership of I.M. Singer & Company.

In 1854 Clark bought Apple Hill, where Judge Nelson had previously lived. Soon after the Civil War he built "Fernleigh" and added extensively to his holdings in the surrounding area. What began as a return to his wife's birthplace as a summer home became an increasingly important interest. Nor did it die with him; his descendants unto the fourth generation came to love the area and to take a very personal interest in its welfare.

An important figure in the transition of Cooperstown from a sleepy Victorian village to a place of national fame was Edward Severin Clark, one of Edward Clark's grandsons. And the irony of his contribution lay in his never being fully aware of all that he had made possible for Cooperstown. Edward Severin Clark is worth our pausing to remember. Those who knew him still speak of him affectionately as "The Squire" and they tell stories about him, for he represented paradoxes which lend themselves to anecdotage. His gardeners and his farm hands used to talk of him endlessly.

"Every morning early he'd be driven all over his estate and to the barns and fields. If he saw sometin' he didn't like, he'd give the fellow responsible a terrible tongue lashing; he'd just blister him. A few hours later he'd be back again—begging the man's pardon, man to man. He was partly crippled, you know, and he couldn't walk very well without help. It must have made him uncommon touchy, seeing other men do simple things he couldn't do. He could get powerful mad, could the Squire, but he was the kindest man I ever worked for."

He had a passion for big things, especially big buildings, and yet he was, for all his wealth, a simple man. He built the huge Otesaga Hotel so that the town would have a fine hotel. The place was a headache in many ways but his rewarding satisfaction came when he sat on the broad porches facing the lake or in the spacious lobby, chatting hour after hour with the guests. He was their host, and having a share in their holiday brought pleasures a more complex person could not have understood. In the winter when the Otesaga was closed, he sat beside the stove in the old Hotel Fenimore, which stood on part of the grounds of Cooper Inn, chiding and chatting with the old-timers who made the spot their gathering place.

He built, in memory of his father, Alfred Corning Clark, a community gymnasium which has become the recreational center of the village. Especially in the winter, it offers recreation for everyone who wants to swim or bowl, play basketball or squash. In the afternoon, after school, it is crowded with youngsters and when dinner is over their places are taken by their fathers and mothers.

Edward Severin Clark, who never married, lived for much of his life on Fenimore Farm, a mile north of the village, in the house that Judge Samuel Nelson and James Fenimore Cooper had occupied before him. In 1918 he built his stone "cow palace," one of the largest and most imposing barns in the state. He had fine cattle, and on summer Sundays, along about milking time, farmers and their families were welcome to come in and see the herd. About 1930 his home on Fenimore Farm was torn down to make room for a new house, built in the Georgian tradition with big white pillars and beautifully balanced wings, designed by Harry St. Clair Zogbaum. He moved into Fenimore House in 1932 and the next year he died. The day he was buried a whole community paid him final, heartfelt tribute.

Edward Severin Clark was the bridge between the elegant and exclusive era that James

Stephen C. Clark, Sr.

Fenimore Cooper predicted and the more democratic era of today. When he died in 1933 the responsibility for his properties fell to his brother, Stephen C. Clark, Sr., who sought to utilize them appropriately and in such a way that they could contribute to the stability and the prosperity of the village. Recognizing the changes taking place in our social and economic system, Stephen Clark gradually evolved uses for the buildings his brother had created which would have a broad base of popular support and appeal, and at the same time be of sound economic and cultural value to the community. Fenimore House was eventually deeded to the New York State Historical Association; the

The Alfred Corning Clark Gymnasium on Main Street, Cooperstown.

Hotel Otesaga, 1909.

Laying the trolley tracks in Cooperstown, about 1900. Below: the trolley on Main Street. The buildings are on the north side of the street. At far left is Ambrose Jordan's house, now Lippitt's; Fenimore Hotel, later demolished; the Mohican Club; the photo studio of Wash Smith and "Putt" Telfer and the S. and F. Uhlman hop office.

Fenimore Farm, predecessor of Fenimore House.

barns came to house The Farmers' Museum; for many years the Otesaga Hotel was rented in the winter to the Knox School; in the 1960s it served as a training center for A.T. and T. personnel. Except for the war years it has been operated as a summer hotel with heavy bookings for conventions. Stephen Clark and his brother, Frederick Ambrose Clark, supplemented the endowment of Cooperstown's Mary Imogene Bassett Hospital, which their brother had established, so that it could become one of the most famous rural medical centers in the country.

These developments, along with the establishment of the Baseball Museum, have altered the historic role of the village. Whereas it had been a charming showpiece, it became a functioning center of medical and historic interest, blessed with the most modern accessories. The effect of increasing thousands of visitors at the museums has become a vitally important factor in the economic structure of the community, for the money spent by these visitors benefits directly or indirectly every person who earns a living in the village. The nostalgic old-timers who complain, as they

General Clinton Canoe Race. The paddlers enter the Susquehanna River as it leaves Lake Otsego.

watch the crowds of summer tourists, that Cooperstown isn't what it used to be, are quite correct. But what they fail to see is that profound economic changes have taken place in the world. In the future the preservation of the culture and traditions of the past can best be safeguarded by a community that is independent and self-reliant.

* * *

Every so often a stranger will stop one of us on the street and ask what it's like to live here all year round. Being modest folk by nature we start out by complaining about the weather: snow and cold for four-and-a-half months and a scientific record for having less sunshine than almost any other place in the country. But, and we pause not wanting to be disloyal, but, we go on, when the sun does shine it's all the more beautiful and appreciated. Snow is very much a part of our lives from Thanksgiving to a late Easter.

In the mid-fifties the Historical Association

started having a ball each February to which the whole town came. It tended toward the formal side, the invitations reading, "the ladies will wear their prettiest and the gentlemen will wear what the ladies think appropriate" or words to that effect. The Susquehanna Ball went on for 20 years but developed into something much bigger, Winter Festival, with auto and dog races on the lake, snow sculpture on Main Street, a number of dances all over town. The lady who first suggested the Susquehanna Ball saw it as a way to raise the spirits in the dark of winter; the Festival carries on that intent on a wider scale.

In the winter time there is usually skiing on Mount Otsego and areas in town are cleared for skating. As already noted, out on the lake north of Pioneer Street stands a colorful colony of fishing shacks. The Concert Series brings a variety of musical events and youngsters go to dancing class one night a week at the gym.

There were years when winter Sundays saw scores of citizens going for a frosty hike under the leadership of "Cap" George Smith, starting at the Village Building and ending at a shack high on Chicken Farm Hill where everybody had hamburgers and hot soup made in a great kettle. Later, in the fifties, Mrs. Stephen C. Clark, Sr., devised a Christmas service which was held in the quarry on Chicken Farm Hill. There was singing by two college choirs, with William Warfield as soloist. Hundreds of people walked up from the village, carrying flashlights and gifts for the manger—the only cars were for the disabled. The icy walls of the quarry reflected the dancing beams of hundreds of little oil lamps. "Adeste Fidelis" never sounded better.

Spring comes very slowly; April can never make up its mind and the tulips wait for May or June. The great spring event is the Governor Clinton Canoe Regatta that starts at dawn on Memorial Day at the spot where the lake gives birth to the Susquehanna. Scores of men and women begin the long seventy-mile rush down the river to Bainbridge. Soon thereafter the big houses open and the high school seniors graduate on the lawn of Fenimore House looking out at the lake, a very high percentage of them headed for college.

Snow sculpture, created during the Winter Carnival.

One of the reasons that so many in Cooperstown and neighboring villages can go on to further education lies with The Clark Foundation and its generous and practical support of promising young people. But the Foundation does much more; it has made possible much of the recent development of the Bassett Hospital, The Farmers' Museum, the New York State Historical Association; it has given vital support to the Fire Department's equipment fund and to the Glimmerglass Opera. Three generations of women in the Clark family have personally concerned themselves very constructively in the physical appearance of the village, especially the flowers that are encouraged around the houses, businesses and public buildings. In recent years the light posts on Main Street have been decked with baskets of flowers and vines. The result is a feeling that flowers are everywhere, giving the town a gaiety that travellers carry away with them, gratefully. Susan Hun Clark, her daughter-in-law, Jane Forbes Clark, and Jane Forbes Clark II have worked tirelessly and anonymously to make this village an ever more beautiful place, and The Clark Foundation has supported their efforts. While the Foundation had been founded by Stephen C. Clark, Sr. and his brother F. Ambrose Clark, the famous sportsman, it was greatly strengthened by their wills and in recent years guided by Stephen C. Clark, Jr.

The Clark Foundation has been one of a growing group of foundations, agencies and individuals who have supported the thriving Glimmerglass Opera Theatre. Founded in 1975 it has attracted highly competent young stars of national reputation to sing in such classics as *La Boheme, Tosca, Manon Lescaut* and such contemporary pieces as Bernstein's *Trouble in Tahiti* and Menotti's *The Medium*, among others. The high quality of the orchestra, many of whose members are also members of The Catskill Symphony in Oneonta, the enthusiastic contributions of workers behind the scenes and in the chorus, and firm, intelligent leadership have created a new cultural force in the area. In the last four years it has tripled its attendance, supporting the statement of a recent critic who wrote, "Glimmerglass has become one of the finest summer opera companies in the land."

A much older organization—going back to 1928—is the Cooperstown Art Association which every year opens an exhibit of paintings, sculpture and crafts. What started as a show of local professional artists has in recent years attracted works from forty-seven states and now is a national and juried show of unusual quality. Activities of the Association continue throughout the year with classes, workshops and demonstrations to encourage the amateurs in the community, to help the creative process to blossom. For many years

Fishing shanties, Lake Otsego, 1925. Styles have changed, the shanties haven't.

A scene from the Glimmerglass Opera Theatre presentation of "La Traviata."

now one painting or sculpture has been bought from each show and those works of art enhance the Library, the Village offices and the County Infirmary.

We shall treat elsewhere such other summer events as the installation of players to the Hall of Fame and the game between the National and American Leagues which bring 10,000 visitors for a single day. And elsewhere, too, we shall describe the Seminars on American Culture at the New York State Historical Association, but all sorts of other activities are underway during the summer months: Sailboat races are a beautiful sight from wherever you watch them and so too are the 4th of July fireworks shot out over the water —cheered and oh'd and ah'd by the thousands who crowd the park and shores.

Our Labor Day comes suddenly. The village seems empty; there are places to park at long last on Main Street and a kind of family joke is repeated over and over, "Well, we got the town back again and no harm done." People pull their boats out of the lake, the docks are partly dismantled. The trees turn to blazing colors by early October, but by election day the trees are bare and we brace ourselves for winter.

In all seasons this is an amiable town to walk in. The Lake and Valley Garden Club has brought out a useful guide for walking tours of the principal historic buildings. The fact is that the village enjoys a wide range of architectural types dating from the 1790s to the present. But the great trees, the ubiquitous flower boxes and gardens, the friendliness of the people, the frequent glimpses of the Lake which changes hues and shadows from minute to minute—all these constants are a factor in telling what it's like to be here all year long.

The Baseball

Traditional Home of Baseball

Updated by WILLIAM J. GUILFOILE

A FRIEND of ours recently returned from a motor trip to the West Coast and he reported that wherever he registered in hotel or tourist camp, the desk clerk invariably looked at the address and commented, "Ah Cooperstown, the home of baseball." And indeed millions of people who never heard of James Fenimore Cooper, nor of Leatherstocking, nor of the Clinton-Sullivan Campaign know Cooperstown as the historic shrine of the baseball world. Its position is made secure by the presence of the National Baseball Hall of Fame and Museum. The two related institutions, housed under one roof, are monuments to the history of the great American game and the greatest of its players.

The late Walter R. Littell, the amiable local historian and for many years the editor simultaneously of both Republican and Democratic papers, enjoyed telling of the beginnings of this greatest of the sports museums. One day in the mid-1930s he happened to mention to his good friend, Stephen C. Clark, Sr., that over in the nearby village of Fly Creek there was a baseball which, according to the traditions of its owners, had been handed down since the days of Abner Doubleday. It is ripped and torn, the stuffing is coming out of its home-made cover, but it symbolizes a century and more of carefree joy in the sandlots and village green. It symbolizes, too, the growth of a great professional sport which binds together in a single enthusiasm Americans of every race and creed, from Wall Street to the hobo jungle. It stands for The Game. You can see it in the Museum of which it was the seed, for when Stephen Clark bought it for a five spot he had unwittingly launched the National Baseball Museum which was opened in 1939—the famous Centennial year when Cooperstown was the scene of the "Cavalcade of Baseball."

June 12, 1939. There's a date to go down in the history of Cooperstown, for on that day, with all the greatest living figures in the baseball world swarming through the streets with fifteen thousand ordinary citizens, the Baseball Museum opened its doors with the fanfare appropriate to the occasion. From Washington came Jim Farley, Postmaster General, with seventy postal clerks, to sell half a million special stamps, bespeaking the Federal Government's official recognition of baseball's hundredth birthday. Along Main Street one could have bumped into Ty Cobb, Walter Johnson, or Eddie Collins, or Tris Speaker, or the great Bambino himself—and their peers. Probably never before nor since were so many popular favorites gathered in one place and they had come to dedicate the place that was to safeguard the relics, the records, and the history of the game that had made them famous.

At noon Main Street was black with humanity. In front of the Museum stood the platform for the notables. Judge Kenesaw Mountain Landis, the Czar of Baseball, appropriately, did the speaking, "Nowhere, other than at its birthplace, could this museum be appropriately situated. To the pioneers who were the moving spirits of the game in its infancy and to the players who have been nominated to the Hall of Fame by the Baseball Writers' Association, we pay just tribute. . . ." When he was finished the music blared "Take me out to the Ball Game," naturally. Then President Ford Frick of the National League and President William Harridge

The Baseball Hall of Fame, original building in 1947.

The Baseball Hall of Fame, with added wings, 1981. Architect Robert S. Hutchins.

of the American League cut the ribbons across the entrance, and the door was unlocked. The names of the "builders of baseball" and six players who had stopped playing before 1900 who had been chosen as the first to be honored in the Hall of Fame were called out over the loudspeakers: George Wright, Morgan C. Bulkeley, Bancroft Johnson, John J. McGraw, Albert G. Spalding, Buck Ewing, Candy Cummings, "Hoss" Radbourne, Cap Anson, Charles Comiskey, Alexander Cartwright and Henry Chadwick. These were the old-timers who, the historians of baseball agreed, had made the modern game what it is.

Then came the moment the crowd had been waiting for, the names of the great ones of whom they had read or travelled to the cities to see play: the living members of the new Hall of Fame who would from that day forth take their places with the pioneers, chosen by the Baseball Writers' Association. When the name of Connie Mack was called the white-haired old manager of the Philadelphia Athletics came through the doors of the Museum that were opened for him. After him, Honus Wagner, Cy Young, George Sisler, Walter Johnson, Napoleon Lajoie, Grover Alexander, Eddie Collins, and as each one came forward to make a short speech and accept a small replica of the plaque on the walls of the Hall of Fame, the roars went up. When Willie Keeler and Christy Mathewson were named others had to accept the replicas for them because they had joined the pioneers.

There was one more to come through the door into the June sunshine and when the Bambino, the Sultan of Swat, the Great Babe Ruth himself stood with the others the crowd, which had loved him and would continue to love him, let out a roar you could hear in Bowerstown. And when he spoke it was of the kids who are the backbone of the game and his memory went back to the days when he was taken off the streets to catch on the team of St. Mary's Industrial School in Baltimore. As always, the Babe had stolen the show.

That afternoon, on Doubleday Field, there was a game in the dress and according to the rules of a century before—a spectacle that was repeated in thousands of cities and villages that year. Then came a real all star game with members of the American and National Leagues on both teams, of which Honus Wagner and Eddie Collins were captains. As baseball, the game was terrible; as showmanship it was terrific and no real follower of baseball will ever forget it.

The two-room museum that opened that day bore little resemblance to today's exciting showcase. In 1950 a wing was added to the facility and the Hall of Fame Gallery was constructed in 1958 to accommodate the bronze plaques. Ten years later the Hall of Fame Library was completed; and a third wing, doubling the size of the entire museum, was opened in 1980. Over 200,000 visitors a year enjoy baseball's ultimate experience.

The origin of the game and the development of the museum are highlighted in the Cooperstown Room, and the Great Moments

Doubleday Field

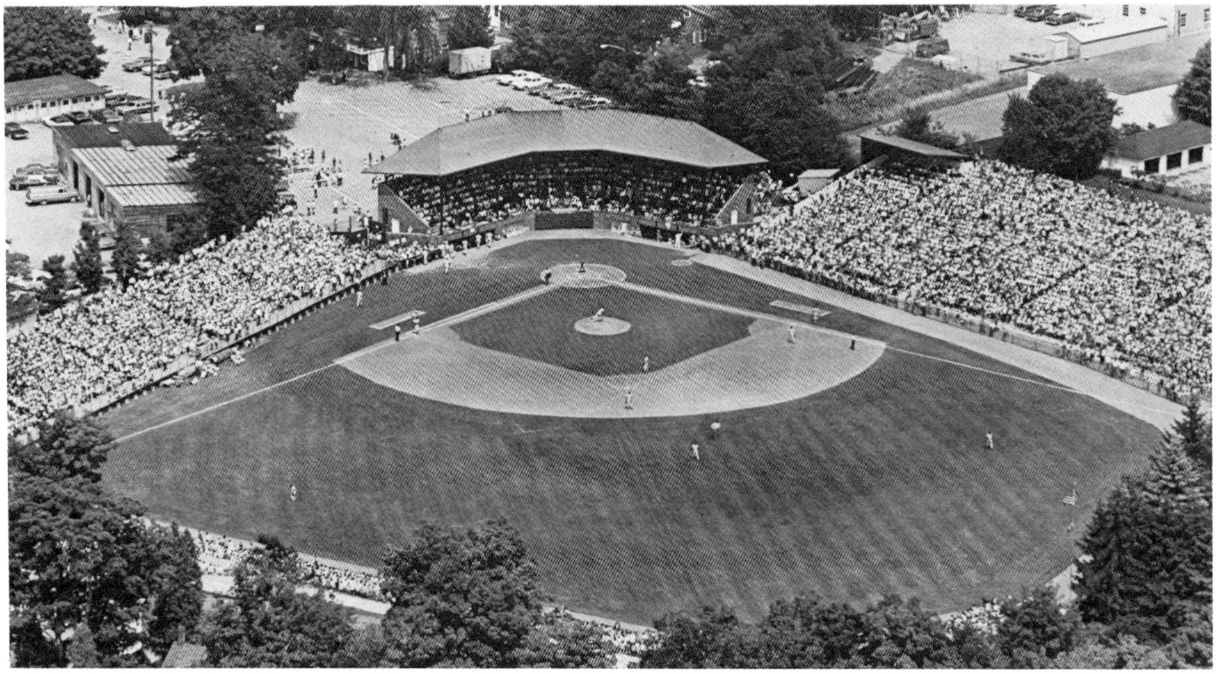

Opening day, 1939. Postmaster General James A. Farley selling commemorative stamps to Ford Frick and Kenesaw Mountain Landis.

Room recalls baseball's unforgettable thrills from Roger Maris's 61st home run to Hank Aaron's 715th. Skillful and artistic use of over 1,000 personal artifacts, photographs and memorabilia present the exciting history of the game from its early forerunner, the English game of rounders, to today's popular teams and favorite players.

Special rooms are devoted to the All-Star Game, baseball's prestigious showcase of the game's top talent, and to the World Series—still the prime sporting event in America. The development of playing equipment over the years and the Babe Ruth and Casey Stengel displays are especially popular among visitors; and in the Ballparks Room, Ebbets Field, the Polo Grounds, Forbes Field, Shibe Park and Crosley Field all come alive once again.

Special areas are devoted to black baseball and to baseball's overseas tours dating back to 1874. The significant roles of the minor leagues and youth baseball are acknowledged, and a unique collection of baseball trading cards attracts the special attention of today's card aficionados.

Today's stars—tomorrow's Hall of Famers—are also well-represented by colorful hanging lobby photos and in the Baseball Today area, where complete uniforms of today's major league teams provide spectacular contrasts. From Abner Doubleday to today's double-knit heroes, it is all presented here in dramatic fashion to delight fans of every age.

Among the more significant artifacts on display are the bat used by Babe Ruth to hit his 60th home run, and that swung by Roger Maris in hitting his 61st; the "Doubleday" baseball—the museum's oldest artifact—and a baseball hurled by Cy Young in registering his 500th career win; the small, almost hand-sized glove used by John McGraw at the turn of the century; Babe Ruth's locker; the bat and ball from Hank Aaron's 714th home run; the bat swung by Bobby Thomson to hit his historic play-off homer in 1951; the mitt used by Yogi Berra to catch Don Larsen's 1956 World Series perfect game; Lou Gehrig's first baseman's glove; Ty Cobb's sliding pads; the bat used by Mickey Mantle to hit his 565-foot, tape-measure home run in Washington; Stan Musial's bats from which he set National League records for hits and RBIs; Ted Williams' bat from his 500th home run; Joe DiMaggio's uniform; the ball thrown by Walter Johnson to record the last out of his 1920 no-hitter against Boston; Honus Wagner's bat and the one used by Willie Mays in collecting his 3000th hit; a bust of Christy Mathewson and the cornerstone from Ebbets Field.

In the Hall of Fame Gallery, each Hall of Famer is honored by a bronze plaque occupying a niche in one of the shrine's alcoves—the greatest honor bestowed on an American athlete.

Two committees have the responsibility of electing new members annually. The Baseball Writers' Association of America considers players who have been active within the past twenty years from the year of election, while the eighteen-man Veterans Committee reviews the qualifications of veteran players, baseball executives, managers, umpires and candidates from the Negro Leagues.

* * *

The story behind the establishment of Cooperstown as the Home of Baseball is in itself an important annal of the sport and of the village. In 1905, as a result of a long standing controversy over the origins of the game, A.G. Spalding, then the head of the sports goods company which bears his name, suggested a commission to study the matter and arrive at an authoritative decision. Seven prominent figures were appointed and in December, 1907, announced their decision. They had heard a good deal of testimony but that which had really impressed them and upon which their decision was based was from one Abner Graves, a mining engineer in his eighties living in Denver. There are three separate letters of Graves, two of them written to the Commission in 1905, and one appearing a dozen years later in Birdsall's *Story of Cooperstown*. Despite minor annoying contradictions, his conclusions are clear enough, namely, that a schoolboy friend of his, Abner Doubleday, who later became a major general in the Civil War, "invented" baseball in Cooperstown some time between 1839 and 1841.

Under the date of April 3, 1905, from Denver, Colorado, Abner Graves wrote the Commission his recollection of the way ball ("town ball") had been played and the changes his boyhood friend, Abner Doubleday, made in the game. In town ball, he said:

> A "tosser" stood beside the home "goal" and tossed the ball straight upward about six feet for the batsman to strike at on its fall, he using a four-inch flat board bat, and all the others who wanted to play being scattered all over the near and far field to catch the ball, the lucky catcher then tak-

Ballparks Room in the new wing.

ing his innings at the bat, while the losing batsman retired to the field. . . . When the batsman struck the ball in the field he would run for an out goal about fifty feet and return, and if the ball was not caught on the fly, and he could return to home goal without getting "plunked" with the ball thrown by anyone, he retained his inning same as in "Old Cat." There being generally from twenty to fifty boys in the field, collisions often occurred in attempt of several to catch the ball.

Abner Doubleday then figured out and made a plan of improvement on Town Ball to limit number of players, and have equal sides; calling it baseball because it had four bases, three being where the runner could rest free of being put out by keeping his feet on the first stone base, while the next on his side took the bat, the first runner being entitled to run whenever he chose, and if he could make home base without being hit by the ball, he tallied. There was a six foot ring within which the pitcher had to stand and toss the ball to the batsman by swinging his hand below his hip. There were pitcher, catcher and two infielders, the two infielders being placed respectively back of the pitcher and between first and second base, and second and third base, and a short distance inside the base lines. The ball used had a rubber center, overwound with yarn, to size some larger than the

Great Moments Room. Nine-foot blow-ups of great baseball events.

present regulation ball, then covered with leather or buckskin, and having plenty of bouncing qualities, wonderful high flies often resulted. Anyone getting the ball was entitled to throw it at a runner and put him out if he could hit him.

On November 17, the same year, he wrote again, apparently in reply to questions from the Commission:

You ask if I can positively name the year of Doubleday's invention, and replying, will say I cannot, although am sure it was either 1839, 1840, and 1841 in the spring of the year when the smaller boys were "playing marbles for keeps," which all stopped when ball commenced, as I remember well Abner Doubleday explaining baseball to a lot of us that were playing marbles in the street, in front of Cooper's tailor shop, and drawing a diagram in the dirt with a stick by marking out a square with a punch mark in each corner for bases, a ring in the center for pitcher, a punch mark just back of home base for catcher, two punch marks of infielders, and four punch marks for outfielders, and we smaller boys didn't like it as it shut us out from playing while Town Ball let in everyone who could run and catch flies, or try to catch them. Then Doubleday drew up same diagram on paper, practically like diagram I will draw on back of another sheet and enclose herewith. The incident has always been associated in my mind with the "Log Cabin and Hard Cider" campaign of General Harrison, my father being a militia captain and rabid partisan of "Old Tippecanoe."

After a description of a game between two Cooperstown schools in 1844 (in which he thought, erroneously, that Doubleday had played), he adds two revealing paragraphs:

Abner Doubleday, I think, was about 16 or 17 years old when he invented the game. He lived in Cooperstown, but I do not know if he was born there. His cousin, John Doubleday (a little younger), was born there, and his father was a merchant with a store at the main four corners in Cooperstown. The Phinneys were running a large bookbindery there, and I believe one in New York at the same time. Of course, it is almost impossible to get documentary proof of the invention, as there is not one chance in ten thousand that a boy's drawing plan of improved ball game would have been preserved for 85 years, as at that time no such interest in games existed as it does now when all items are printed and societies and clubs preserve everything.

And finally, in Birdsall's book, there is another direct quotation from Graves which further supplements these:

Abner Doubleday was several years older than I. In 1838 and 1839 I was attending the "Frog Hollow" school south of the Presbyterian Church, while he was at school somewhere on the hill. I do not know, neither is it possible for anyone to know, on what spot the first game of Base Ball was played according to Doubleday's plan. He went diligently among the boys in the town, and in several schools, explaining the plan, and inducing them to play Base Ball in lieu of the other games. Doubleday's game was played in a good many places around town: sometimes in the old militia muster lot, or training ground, a couple of hundred yards southeasterly from the Court House, where County Fairs were occasionally held [Doubleday Field]: sometimes in Mr. Bennett's field south of Otsego Academy [site of St. Mary's Church parish house]: at other times over in the Miller's Bay neighborhood [Country Club grounds], and up the Lake.

These reports give evidence of coming from a physically active and mentally sharp old man, who, on three separate occasions set down statements which, in their major points, agree. That he was in error in the matter of dates is undeniable; there is reason to believe that he confused the Harrison campaign of 1836 with that of 1840, for Doubleday entered West Point in 1838 to stay until his graduation in 1842. We know from a *History of Otsego County*, published in 1878, that he had re-

Hall of Fame Gallery where each Hall of Famer is represented by a bronze plaque. Below: Babe Ruth's plaque.

ceived preparatory education in Cooperstown, but in which school, there is, as yet, no way of knowing. Read objectively, Graves' testimony gives the impression of being an honest, factual statement and much of the internal evidence strengthens rather than weakens his case.

In recent years Graves' testimony and the decision of the Commission have been attacked by some of the historians of the game. Briefly stated, their position is that the name "baseball" had been in popular use in the United States since early in the decade of the 1830s; that rules printed in 1834 indicate that Doubleday (who never made any claim for himself regarding baseball nor showed any particular interest in it) did not invent the game; that the diamond shaped field had been shown in illustrations as early as 1829 in *The Boy's Own Book*; that the team system and the limitation of numbers are also to be found in print before 1839.

All of this is incontrovertible and yet Graves' testimony regarding the events he witnessed stands unimpaired. The only ques-

The Babe Ruth Exhibit. In the photo, Ruth is shown in his automobile with Yankee manager Miller Huggins.

tion involved is whether Doubleday was the first person to combine at one time and in one place the various elements which represented the change from town ball to baseball. Historians of the game may well decide when all the evidence is gathered that Graves' testimony, covering a period when a widely played game (town ball) was undergoing rapid changes all over the country, captures a point in time when these changes arrived in one typical American community and caused a minor revolution on the sandlot.

But these are problems for the future and far into the future Cooperstown will remain the Home of Baseball because the report of the 1907 Commission and the National Baseball Museum and the Hall of Fame have made it the historic capital of the Game.

The Mary Imogene Bassett Hospital

By Clinton Van Zandt Hawn, M.D.

A PORTRAIT hangs on the wall of the out-patient lobby of the Mary Imogene Bassett Hospital.* It depicts the woman for whom the hospital was named, a handsome, stately, resolute woman with commanding blue eyes, dressed in a blue tailored suit, and carrying the small black bag of the practicing physician. She was this, as were her parents. Born in Mount Vision, a few miles from Cooperstown, in 1856 to Doctors Wilson T. and Mary Augusta Bassett, Mary Imogene moved with them to Cooperstown in 1874. Her father and mother moved to Cooperstown because of a growing medical practice. They purchased the three-storied brick house, Otsego Mansion, on lower Fair Street, and fitted it out for "the reception of patients," charging "$6. to $12. a week, including board and treatment."

At a time when few women found recognition in medical careers, Dr. Bassett distinguished herself early. Although she was thirty-one years old when she was graduated from the Woman's Medical College of Pennsylvania in 1887, she sought further training and became an Instructor in Nervous Diseases at the Philadelphia Polyclinic and College for Graduates in Medicine. She also served as assistant to a well-known neurologist. Soon she became the author of several articles published in that field. Her enterprise and competence were recognized by her peers; she was elected delegate to the Philadelphia County Medical Society and to the American Medical Association in the following year. From these noteworthy beginnings in academic medicine and in medical organization she turned abruptly to a village and rural general practice with her aging father after the death of her mother in 1893.

Dr. Wilson Bassett died in 1905 and his daughter continued alone. Hers was an active practice in the village and countryside. She conducted it unselfishly, wisely and sympathetically bringing her understanding and considerable skills to the sick and needy. "Doctor Molly" had but little leisure; her career was her life.

Among her friends and patients was Edward Severin Clark, "The Squire." He came to have great admiration for the diligence, competence and spirit of this woman. According to anecdote, he heard her express a wish for a laboratory to provide scientific data with which she and the other practitioners of the village might better care for their patients. Mr. Clark granted her wish, while his architect elaborated upon it. The result was a handsome small hospital constructed of native fieldstone and equipped with the best that was available. It bore her name to honor her while living, an unusual touch. The hospital, nearing completion in 1918, was offered by Mr. Clark to the United States Army as a convalescent home for aviation officers. It was so used until late the following year. The opening to the public came in June 1922, with Dr. Bassett serving as chief of staff. Tragically and suddenly she died of a stroke at home in October of that year. Mr. Clark directed that the light in the cupola of the hospital should burn through each night in memory of her.

*EYE-mo-gene was the pronunciation preferred by Dr. Mary Imogene Bassett.

Dr. Mary Imogene Bassett

Dr. Mary A. Bassett and Dr. Wilson T. Bassett.

There were physicians in Cooperstown from its beginnings, almost as soon as there were lawyers. Records show three in 1790. As noted in an earlier chapter, one of these was banished for having mixed an emetic with the punch served at a ball in the Red Lion Inn. A druggist came in 1801. His sign stated: "Itch cured for 2 cts. 4 cts. 6 cts. Unguentum, Walk In."

The practice of medicine in the first half of the nineteenth century in Cooperstown was much like that in villages throughout the United States—well-intended but with minimal scientific background. The Civil War brought advances. A memorable contribution to medical practice in the village was the founding of the first hospital, the Thanksgiving Hospital. This had its origin in the active mind of that concerned, public-spirited woman, Miss Susan Fenimore Cooper, daughter of the novelist. It was established in 1868 in gratitude for the ending of the Civil War but it was forced to close eight years later because of financial problems. A generous endowment by Alfred Corning Clark permitted the hospital to reopen in 1889, and to move to new quarters in 1896, where it had 15 beds, increased to 25 beds in 1905. Here it served its mission until it was succeeded by the Mary Imogene Bassett Hospital. Currently it is a gracious retirement dwelling, The Clara Welch Thanksgiving Home on Grove St.

After the untimely death of Dr. Bassett the hospital soon found itself in financial difficulties. One hundred beds were far too many to be filled from the practices of the physicians of the village. Leadership was not forthcoming. Reluctantly it was decided to close the hospital in 1925.

Not long thereafter, idealistic and well-trained young physicians associated with the Presbyterian Hospital of the City of New York expressed interest in developing a group practice in a rural community. They were encouraged by a colleague, Dr. Henry S. Fenimore Cooper of this village, then residing in New York. He arranged for them to meet Mr. Stephen C. Clark, Sr., who became interested in the concept. With his backing and that of his brother, Mr. Edward Severin Clark, the hospital was reopened in March 1927.

The reopening was hailed in *The Knickerbocker Press* of Albany, N.Y., January 1, 1928, as a "novel experiment being successfully conducted." Dr. James Greenough, a young but experienced surgeon, was the director and spokesman for the newspaper interview. He stated the goals of the "Cooperstown plan." Four local physicians had been included in the attending staff and offices for them had been provided in the hospital. Salaries for all members of the staff were established, an important but unusual feature. There were four wards consisting of eight beds each, twenty private rooms, and nine semi-private rooms, each accommodating two patients. Thirty registered nurses cared for the patients and a nurse's training school was planned for the future. The medical library functioned from the start and was being augmented constantly. The hospital was splendidly equipped; for example, in the basement was housed 500 mg. of radium for the treatment of cancer. It was said to be the largest amount between Buffalo and New York City.

The buildings, constructed as they were of grey fieldstone, were described as forming "one of the handsomest structures in New York State," and a "showplace of the Town." These were *not* humble beginnings.

Dr. George M. Mackenzie, the article noted, had been formerly Assistant Professor of Medicine at Columbia University and was now head of the Laboratory and medical departments. He and Dr. Greenough were on the board of directors of the hospital. The "Cooperstown plan" had received state approval and a charter. There were two interns; appropriately, one was a young woman. A pediatrician was to join the staff on July 1, 1928. The four local physicians were encouraged to develop their special interests.

Dr. Greenough left the group in 1929 and entered private practice in nearby Oneonta; he was later elected President of the New York State Medical Society.

Dr. Mackenzie became Director as well as Physician-in-Chief and proved to be a man of extraordinary vision. He early stated the relationship of the hospital group to the community to preclude misunderstanding about the referral of patients. "When the doctor of choice deems it advisable he refers the patient, *with the patient's consent*, to the physician better able to care for him."

A noteworthy statement of purposes of the hospital followed: "With our splendid equipment and generous backing we have the opportunity to develop an institution devoted to giving patients the best possible medical and surgical treatment by a staff familiar with the rapidly developing and rapidly changing science of medicine; to function as a focus in a rural district for dissemination of information. . . to contribute even in a small way to the progress of medicine and surgery. . . , to offer to the physicians of the region. . . facilities for the study and care of their patients." Thus were enunciated the basic principles that have guided the hospital ever since.

In 1931 a bold new concept was implemented with the approval of the Board of Medical Examiners of the State of New York.

The Bassett Hospital Annual Payment Plan was a forerunner of plans for prepaid medical and surgical care, such as Blue Cross, Blue Shield and the like. The Annual Payment Plan was to prove practicable over the next ten years. It was discontinued on the recommendation of state officials who favored the development of a regional plan. Opposition to the Bassett plan was expressed when it originated but the popularity and validity of these plans has long since been established.

The educational role of the hospital was also established early. In 1930–31 there were two medical interns and one each in surgery and pediatrics. The College of Physicians and Surgeons of Columbia University, Harvard Medical School and Johns Hopkins University were represented by their graduates. Medical students came informally in the summer to study. The hospital thus became a teaching institution.

In 1932 the Advisory Board was composed of Professors of Medicine, Surgery and Deans from Columbia, Johns Hopkins and Albany Medical College.

Dr. Mackenzie reported with pride: "The old lecture room with its vaulted ceiling and high windows lends itself to the new library. Current magazines, books and bound periodicals of the past ten years are kept here within easy reach of the professional staff." The development of a remarkable library has

Staff of Bassett Hospital, 1920s. Front row, left to right, Drs. Floyd J. Atwell, George M. Mackenzie, James Greenough, Charles W. Lanning, Harry L. Cruttenden. Rear, Frederick M. Johnson, Dorothy Loynes and Abbott W. Allen.

Bassett Hospital as it appeared in 1948.

come about in the ensuing years. Certainly the library is one of his great legacies, and one that is without equal in community hospitals or in many teaching hospitals.

Although the depression of the thirties was felt in Cooperstown and in the surrounding areas the operating deficit of the hospital was met by funds provided by Mr. Edward Severin Clark and by the Clark and Scriven Foundations, and the hospital was not forced to curtail its activities in providing health care and medical education. Members of the staff were encouraged to take leaves of absence to increase their knowledge of newer aspects of medical care. A small laboratory for surgical research was opened. The informal affiliation with Columbia University for teaching medical students was continued and strengthened.

In 1938 it was pointed out by Dr. Lowell Reed, Dean of the School of Hygiene of Johns Hopkins University, and a preeminent biostatistician, that nowhere else were there data assembled that made possible an accurate picture of morbidity in a rural area. Accurate and informative charts had been kept on the 15,000 admissions from 1928 to

1938. From the impetus given by Dr. Reed and energetically developed by Dr. Mackenzie, a conference on several phases of rural medicine was held in October, 1938. Present were many distinguished public officials and interested private citizens. They addressed themselves to problems of morbidity and economics of rural medicine. Health departments, school health programs and post-graduate education in rural areas were considered. The collected papers presented at this conference were published.

The exigencies of the war years forced the curtailment of many activities. Despite the times, clinical research continued. Dr. John H. Powers, Associate Surgeon, presented his obervations of the early ambulation of post-operative patients to official Washington. The reduction of complications was significant as was the length of hospitalization in this group. This contribution was recognized widely both in the medical profession and by the general public.

A major change in the organization of the hospital came about the year after the war ended. From 1927 to 1946 funds to meet the budgeted operating deficit of the hospital had been provided, first by Mr. Edward Severin Clark and then by the Clark and Scriven Foundation, as we have noted. In April, 1946 the Boards of Directors of those foundations established the hospital as a permanent endowed public institution "for the care of the sick, for medical research, and medical education." The final step in the affiliation with Columbia came about by joint action of the Boards of Trustees of the institutions involved. Academic status was bestowed on the hospital and the members of its staff.

In 1947 Dr. Mackenzie retired, leaving a living testimony to his vision of "cooperatively organized intelligence"—a hospital-based group medical practice with opportunities for continuing medical growth, research and teaching. Five years later he died. Many tributes were paid to this man whose knowledge of medicine, keen awareness of its trends, and remarkable energy together with the exceptional backing of the Trustees produced the fine teaching hospital that Bassett has become. A lasting memorial may be seen in the library where there is a first-rate portrait of this man. A plaque beneath is inscribed

TO HONOR

GEORGE MINER MACKENZIE, M.D.
FOR A SCORE OF YEARS
PHYSICIAN-IN-CHIEF AND DIRECTOR
RESOLUTE LEADER AND MEDICAL PIONEER
WHOSE INSPIRATION CREATED THIS LIBRARY
MAY ALL READERS HERE HOLD HIM
IN GRATEFUL REMEMBRANCE.

* * *

Dr. James Bordley III was appointed Physician-in-Chief and Director. He was a graduate of Yale University and Johns Hopkins University Medical School. There had been depletion of the hospital staff and new appointments were made by Dr. Bordley to bring it back to full strength, fifteen. There was no slackening in the demands for medical services, however. It had become apparent that expansion was necessary. The Bassett Hospital had been designated a "secondary center" for medical care in Otsego and Delaware Counties. A fifty percent expansion of bed capacity was recommended by the New York State Department of Health. It was also apparent that lack of laboratory space and proper quarters for laboratory animals were serious obstacles to planning research. The handsome hospital buildings of the 1920s were inadequate for the patient needs and ancillary services of 1947.

In 1950 construction was begun of a new building and for modernization of existing buildings with funds provided by the Clark and Scriven Foundations and by a federal grant under the Hill-Burton Act. This three-storied structure was to connect with the existing buildings bringing all "under one roof." It provided new operating rooms, laboratories and offices as well as x-ray facilities. Thirty additional beds for inpatients resulted from rearrangement of space.

The problems of comparing the operating costs of a fully-equipped teaching hospital with those of other hospitals in the area were noted in 1951 in the *Director's Annual Report* which ". . . inevitably records an expression of concern about the economic factors which are continually undermining the budgetary structure." This was to be a recurring theme down to the present.

The new building was completed, at long last, and appropriately dedicated in 1954. Community nursing had been established the previous year with a Home Care Program. In 1955, with the aid of a grant from the Commonwealth Fund, a department of psychiatry was established. This was a pioneering effort. The acceptance of this medical specialty by a rural community was questioned, but it succeeded. In 1956 it was noted that 44 percent of hospital admissions came from outside Otsego County. Home visits and office visits were 60 percent more than in 1946.

With the pressures of the hospital expansion and the increase in the complexity of administration, Dr. Bordley chose to relinquish his clinical and teaching responsibilities to a separate Physician-in-Chief and to concentrate on being the Director. He felt that the presence of new and remodelled community hospitals in the region would provide improved basic medical care. Therefore the

Bassett Hospital with the 1954 additions.

future of Bassett Hospital lay in making available to the region specialized services resulting from the increased specialization of the medical practice in addition to providing the basic care needed by the people of the village and environs. He noted that the hospital had become a "rural medical center with more than a local influence and more than a local responsibility."

In the post-war period, encouragement of research by the federal government in the form of grants by the United States Public Health Service resulted in a massive infusion of financial support, nationwide. The Bassett Hospital received its share. In 1957 the total operating income was reported as $1.2 million; research grants from government and other sources approached $0.5 million.

The interest of several members of the staff in studying the possibilities of storing and subsequently transplanting bone marrow for the treatment of radiated leukemic patients led to the construction of an annex, the Cobalt Teletherapy Unit. This housed radioactive Cobalt-60 sources for delivering total body radiation. The concept was bold; the success, partial. This project brought national, even international recognition and the hospital became known as a pioneering institution in the complex treatment of radiation injury. An addition of two stories upon the new west wing was built with funds provided in a grant from the United States Public Health Service. It was to house laboratories for the burgeoning research activities.

In his report for 1960, Dr. Bordley chronicled the passing of Mr. Stephen C. Clark, Sr. who had shown great vision in supporting Dr. George Mackenzie's revolutionary concept of an ideal rural hospital. Mr. Clark was also a strong advocate and supporter of scientific investigation. In his will he established a substantial fund for the endowment of research at the hospital. A fund to facilitate the efforts of Dr. T. Campbell Goodwin and Dr. Mary Goodwin, then the pediatricians, in providing comprehensive care for the children of this and neighboring communities was also established. Mr. Clark had early recognized that Cooperstown must become self-sustaining and he envisioned a strong role of the hospital in the local economy.

The cupola with its light for Dr. Bassett.

The Trustees sought advice in formulating a long-range plan. A hospital consulting firm was chosen. The outmoded building for inpatients was deemed no longer suitable. It was to be vacated and a new structure built to double the bed capacity and to provide new service laboratories, x-ray department, pharmacy, business offices, operating rooms and cafeteria. Plans were well under way when Dr. Bordley retired at the end of 1966, and the next July saw ground broken for the new building. Dr. Douglas Damrosch succeeded Dr. Bordley, but he soon returned to a more academic position at Columbia in October 1967.

* * *

The next, and current, Director was Dr. Charles A. Ashley. He is a graduate of Cornell University and its medical school, and served his internship at the Bassett Hospital. After residency and post-graduate training elsewhere he returned in 1955 as Associate Pathologist of the Mary Imogene Bassett Hospital. From a promising career as an investigator he was diverted into administration, bringing to the position a knowledge of the workings of the hospital acquired first-hand. Early in his directorship a consultant was retained to study the needs of the out-patient services and to make recommendations to the Trustees for their development. There continued to be a sizable increase in the number of patients coming from outside Otsego County. In 1969 there were 60,000 visits to the out-patient department; in 1971, 83,000.

Financial problems again appeared. At the end of 1969 the Cost Control Law in New York State made the creation of a budget for

The late Dr. James Bordley III and Mrs. Bordley before his portrait by Everett Raymond Kinstler.

Bassett Hospital as it is today.

the ensuing year difficult if not impossible for every hospital in the state. Further, reimbursement by the state for the care of Medicaid patients and those enrolled in Blue Cross was limited by rigid formula and proved to be less than actual cost for the teaching hospitals with their considerable expenses for highly specialized care.

An unsolicited but highly complimentary report by the Carnegie Foundation in 1971 cited the Bassett Hospital as an existing institution to serve as a model for regional centers recommended for the nation in *Higher Education and the Nation's Health Policies for Medical and Dental Education.*

The problem of providing medical care in nearby communities unable to recruit the "vanishing" general practitioner was partially solved by establishing Nurse Practitioners, with Bassett Hospital-based physicians immediately available by telephone for consultation and referral, if necessary. This was an innovative approach to an ever growing shortage of physicians in rural areas. The first hospital-associated health care center was opened in 1974; the second, four years later.

With the malpractice insurance crisis in New York State came the drastic rise in the cost to the hospital for coverage of its staff members, from $89,000 to $1,080,000 in just two years. To counter this, the Trustees established a system of self-insurance with an appropriate reserve fund, in 1977.

In his report for the year 1980, the Director commented that in twelve years of his tenure the physical plant had doubled in size, doubled in the number of employees, more than doubled in medical staff, and doubled in the number of outpatient visits and in days of inpatient care provided. It was time to enlarge the administration and to make appropriate changes in internal governance. Dealing with the complexities and vagaries of state and federal agencies had become increasingly time consuming.

* * *

This account of the development of this unusual hospital has concerned itself primarily with the implementation of ideas and ideals as they were shaped and expressed at the beginning. Hospital-based group practice, originally an anathema to some, has been widely accepted. Patient-physician relationships have not been sacrificed. That the atmosphere is conducive to clinical and laboratory research is attested by many and diverse articles published over the years. Certain investigations have brought national and international acclaim. There are currently five *full-time* investigators at the doctoral level, studying basic problems in biochemistry and immunology. The annual research budget approaches one million dollars, but this is only 3 percent of the total hospital operating cost and is defrayed by outside grants in addition to the Stephen C. Clark Research Fund.

As a teaching institution, Bassett Hospital, by the end of 1980, had served 471 interns who received post-graduate training here as had 318 residents and fellows. Literally hundreds of medical students from many universities had spent one or more months "at the Bassett." Full-time staff now number more than seventy. The medical library collection is large and much used. There are in excess of 30,000 bound volumes and 500 periodicals.

In 1930 there were fewer than 100 employees; in 1980, there were over 1000. Truly, the hospital had become of considerable economic importance in the area. A major medical center with all its appurtenances had evolved.

* * *

In the entrance to the lobby where hangs the portrait of Dr. Bassett there are two plaques:

TO THE MEMORY OF
STEPHEN CARLTON CLARK
A GREAT MAN AND A GOOD MAN
WHOSE MONUMENT IS
ALL THAT HE DID
IN THE SERVICE OF COOPERSTOWN
AND FOR HIS FELLOW CITIZENS
EVERYWHERE

TO THE MEMORY OF
EDWARD SEVERIN CLARK
WHO FOUNDED THIS HOSPITAL
AND NAMED IT FOR
DR. MARY IMOGENE BASSETT
THAT HER LIFE OF DEVOTED SERVICE
MIGHT SERVE AS AN INSPIRATION
TO THOSE WHO LABOR HERE
TO SERVE MANKIND.

A Center for History
The Association

A MILE north of the village, after passing the greensward of the golf course with its backdrop of lake and tree-covered ridge, one comes to a remarkable complex of institutions and activities concerned with interpreting the American past. A historical society, two museums, a research library and two graduate programs comprise an overall institution serving the educational needs of school children, average citizens, informed amateur historians, research scholars, and graduate students interested in careers in history museums or in the conservation of artistic and historic objects.

At the core of this complex is the New York State Historical Association, founded in 1899, brought to Cooperstown from Ticonderoga at the invitation of Stephen C. Clark, Sr. in 1939. At first it occupied the Village Building on Main Street but in 1945 it moved to Fenimore House which was transformed into a museum of upstate New York art. The building was also the operative headquarters of the increasingly active Association. During the 1930s, under the presidency of Dixon Ryan Fox, and in conjunction with Columbia University Press, the Association had published the ten-volume *History of New York*, edited by Alexander C. Flick, and a number of monographs, including Arthur C. Parker's pioneering *Manual for History Museums*. The Association began to reach out in a variety of fresh experiments to see how best it could serve its constituency.

In the 1930s most historical societies saw their constituencies as very narrow ones; at Cooperstown there were to be no limits. When the State Education Department rewrote the social studies syllabus to include the history of New York State, the Association set up a Junior Program, very creatively led by Mary E. Cunningham, who organized chapters in junior high schools all over the state and brought out a magazine for these young members, called *The Yorker*. As soon as the war was over, she held the first Yorker convention, which became an annual event, bringing hundreds of history-minded youngsters together for a day of talks and historical exhibits and youthful politicking. For forty years, this program, supplemented with travelling exhibits, visits to museums (Cooperstown's especially), workshops, conferences for teachers and chapter leaders have put a stamp on the historical thinking of three generations of our citizens.

After World War II was over there was a ground swell of interest in all aspects of the American past among average citizens. These were people who yearned for guidance in their reading and their thinking. To meet that need, the Seminars on American Culture began in 1948 to offer an adult education experience with topflight authorities who were also articulate and interesting. They taught such subjects as New York's history and folklife and folklore, genealogy; they sought to inform and professionalize the volunteer workers in historical societies, museums and libraries. A third of a century later, the first weeks of July still see a couple of hundred adults learning about the subjects that have become avocations of great import to the quality of their lives.

Seminars on American Culture. A class in Early House Framing, above, and lunch in the tent.

Fenimore House, home of the New York State Historical Association.

The step that rounded out the educational mission of the Association came in 1964 when it joined hands with the State University of New York College at Oneonta to open two Cooperstown Graduate Programs offering a Master of Arts degree—one to prepare personnel for leadership in history museums of all kinds, and a second to study folk life in depth; in 1970 a third program was added to teach the conservation of historic and artistic objects. The collections and exhibits of both Fenimore House and The Farmers' Museum became laboratories for students; in return, their researches greatly enriched the understanding of the collections. Students worked with the museum objects in hand, learning to study and analyze the material object as a document. Students came to these programs from all over this country and Canada and left to serve museums and cultural agencies in every state of the Union. In 1979 the Folk Culture Program was dropped, but the two remaining programs are thriving.

Perhaps more than anything else, the Seminars and Graduate Programs established the Association as a frontrunner among the nation's historical agencies, but publications, library and museums provided the solid

Eel Spearing at Setauket. *Oil on canvas by William Sidney Mount, 1845.*

foundation which made all else possible.

New York History is the Association's quarterly journal for historians and its long shelf of annual volumes represent a major contribution to the scholarship of the state's history. But the Cooperstown years have also produced a one-volume history of New York, Jared Van Wagenen's *Golden Age of Homespun, A Bibliography of Newspapers in Fourteen New York Counties*, and other titles.

Since 1969, the Kerr History Prize, endowed by Mr. Paul S. Kerr and named for him by the Association's trustees, has honored the best article appearing each year in *New York History*. The New York State Historical Association Manuscript Award was created in 1974 and offers a cash award and assistance in publication to the best book-length work dealing with New York history. Each of the winners thus far has been published by a major university press.

Originally the library was in one room in

Robert Fulton's portrait by Benjamin West.

Joseph Brant. Oil on canvas by Gilbert Stuart, 1786.

Fenimore House, then two rooms, then a wing, but in 1968, through the generous understanding of the Clark Foundation, a new building was added to the complex. Three floors of open stacks, a large classroom, audio-visual equipment, and a room for special collections provided a splendid tool for scholarship. The book collections of three New York scholars and writers were purchased in the 1960s: those of Roger Butterfield, Carl Carmer and Harold W. Thompson. These strengthened the holdings immeasurably—Butterfield especially in early pictorial journals and runs of historical publications; Carmer in obscure publications of New York's past, books that had contributed to *Listen for a Lonesome Drum, Dark Trees to the Wind* and others of his volumes; and Thompson in a classical selection of books on American folklore. There also came Thompson's mammoth manuscript

Gilbert Stuart

collection of folklore garnered by his students at Albany and Cornell over a quarter of a century. This collection has been supplemented by manuscript collections and tape recordings made by students of the Cooperstown Graduate Programs.

Good accessions in a library or a museum attract other good accessions so that letters, diaries, account books soon filled the room for special collections. Florence Ward, the registrar for many years, had been collecting early photographs of nearly every house in Cooperstown and related clippings, long before she came to work at Fenimore House; that collection also came to the library. Books relating to exhibits in Fenimore House and in The Farmers' Museum, books related to teaching in the Graduate Programs and Seminars combined to produce a research library filled with the resources and the tools that make scholarship possible in the right hands.

Marquis de Lafayette. These bronze busts were cast from life masks made by J.H.I. Browere when Lafayette was sixty-seven and Stuart was seventy.

Fenimore House

The handsome stone house that Harry St. Clair Zogbaum designed for Edward Severin Clark proved to be remarkably adaptable for a museum. The rooms were large and high and problems of traffic flow solved themselves naturally. There was room for seventeen galleries—some unusually large, and a great attic for storage and office space for a sizable staff.

Stephen C. Clark, Sr. over a long lifetime had developed a connoiseur's taste in art and from 1939 on he bought for the Association, New York State landscapes, genres, and portraits by masters of their time. Visitors have different favorites but William Sidney Mount's "Eel Spearing," Thomas Cole's "Last of the Mohicans," Benjamin West's portrait of Robert Fulton and Gilbert Stuart's "Joseph Brant" have always been rated highly, along with scores of others. Recently, Dr. Henry S. Fenimore Cooper gave to the Association Gilbert Stuart's portrait of his great-great-grandfather, Judge William Cooper, and John Wesley Jarvis's portrait of James Fenimore Cooper, along with a number of other paintings and objects of the Cooper family. These gifts led to a major permanent exhibit concerned with the novelist, his father and family, and included paintings of scenes from his novels which had long been in the collection. An adjacent gallery is devoted to his and his father's acquaintances and friends.

Some of these friends had had life masks rendered by a secret process developed by a man of many parts named J.H.I. Browere. Browere had in mind a gallery of masks of founders of the Republic but it did not come to pass till long after his death when Mr. Clark bought seventeen of them and had them cast in bronze for the Association. Perhaps the most striking of Cooper's friends represented in this collection is the Marquis de Lafayette, but all the masks give a special kind of insight to the sitter. Thomas Jefferson, John and John Quincy Adams, DeWitt Clinton, and a slightly frumpy but good-natured Dolly Madison are among those in the collection.

Recent years have seen a remarkable growth of interest in the arts that were created outside the academic tradition, known rather loosely as American folk art. The major collection of the latter at Fenimore House has played a considerable part in that interest. On three occasions Mr. Clark made major purchases of folk art for the collection: He bought thirteen pieces of the Nadelman collection in 1948, the collection of Jean and Howard Lipman in 1949 and ten years later the exclusive collection of paintings accumulated by Mr. and Mrs. William Gunn. A great many single items have been acquired in the intervening years until practically every type of American folk art is represented.

The collection of folk art covers nearly two and a half centuries; the earliest and most important piece is the 1733 Van Bergen Overmantel, a seven-foot pair of boards on which Martin Van Bergen, a wealthy Hudson Valley Dutch farmer, had a painter named John

The Van Bergen Overmantel, *attributed to John Heaton, ca. 1733.*

Heaton paint the Van Bergen's new house, their barn and hay barrack, the entire family of nine plus Van Bergen's brother and two nephews, two indentured servants, four slaves and horses, cows, sheep, and a barnyard fowl. It is the earliest conversation piece, the earliest landscape of the Catskills and the only visual document that exists describing everyday life in rural Dutch New York.

At the other end of the spectrum are twentieth-century artists like the carver John Scholl, a house carpenter who, in his later years, whittled out marvelous abstract snow drops, three feet across, or like Edgar Tolson whose carved scenes of Adam and Eve in and out of the Garden of Eden are represented by a scene of the temptation charged with unhappy portent.

Representing the nineteenth and twentieth centuries down to the present time are ship's figureheads, quilts of blazing color and strong design, weathervanes of Indians, fish and cocks, trade signs of Indian maidens, stylish ladies, classical figures, and one of the earliest cigar store figures, carved by a slave named Job, which strongly reflects the carving style of West Africa. There are hundreds of pictures in many media, portraits, landscapes and genres. The work of itinerant portraitists like John Brewster, William Matthew Prior, and Joseph W. Stock and the work of more settled painters like Joseph Hidley and Grandma Moses.

There are many styles, many techniques in a collection as catholic as this one but there are certain qualities that comprise a common denominator: vigor, a strong sense of design, bright rather than subtle colors, interesting idiosyncratic solutions to such problems as perspective, composition and modeling. In a world that has come to appreciate cave paintings, African primitive art, Eskimo carvings, there is a place for the instinctively creative works of our non-academic artists, a place capable of giving a great deal of pleasure.

In 1853, fourteen years after Daguerre invented the photograph, a man who had been an itinerant photographer settled down to do business in Cooperstown. This was Washington G. Smith who stayed in business until his death in 1893. About 1887 he took into partnership Arthur S. Telfer who shot his last photograph in 1953 at the age of 94. Both of these men used glass plate negatives and some 55,000 of these came into the possession of the Association in the late 1940s. They contain a photographic record of a village, its festivals, its funerals, its weddings, work, play,

Peaceable Kingdom, *by Edward Hicks, ca. 1840–1845.*

storms and sunshine over a full century. And always the faces of our people, babies to octogenarians, face after face.

This became the basis for a very large photographic archive which has later been augmented by the negatives and photographs of local amateur photographers like Charles Zabriskie, Folger Oudin, Sr. and others. In 1978 the Association opened a major exhibit of the Smith-Telfer collection, at which time a volume, *The Smith and Telfer Photographic Collection* was published.

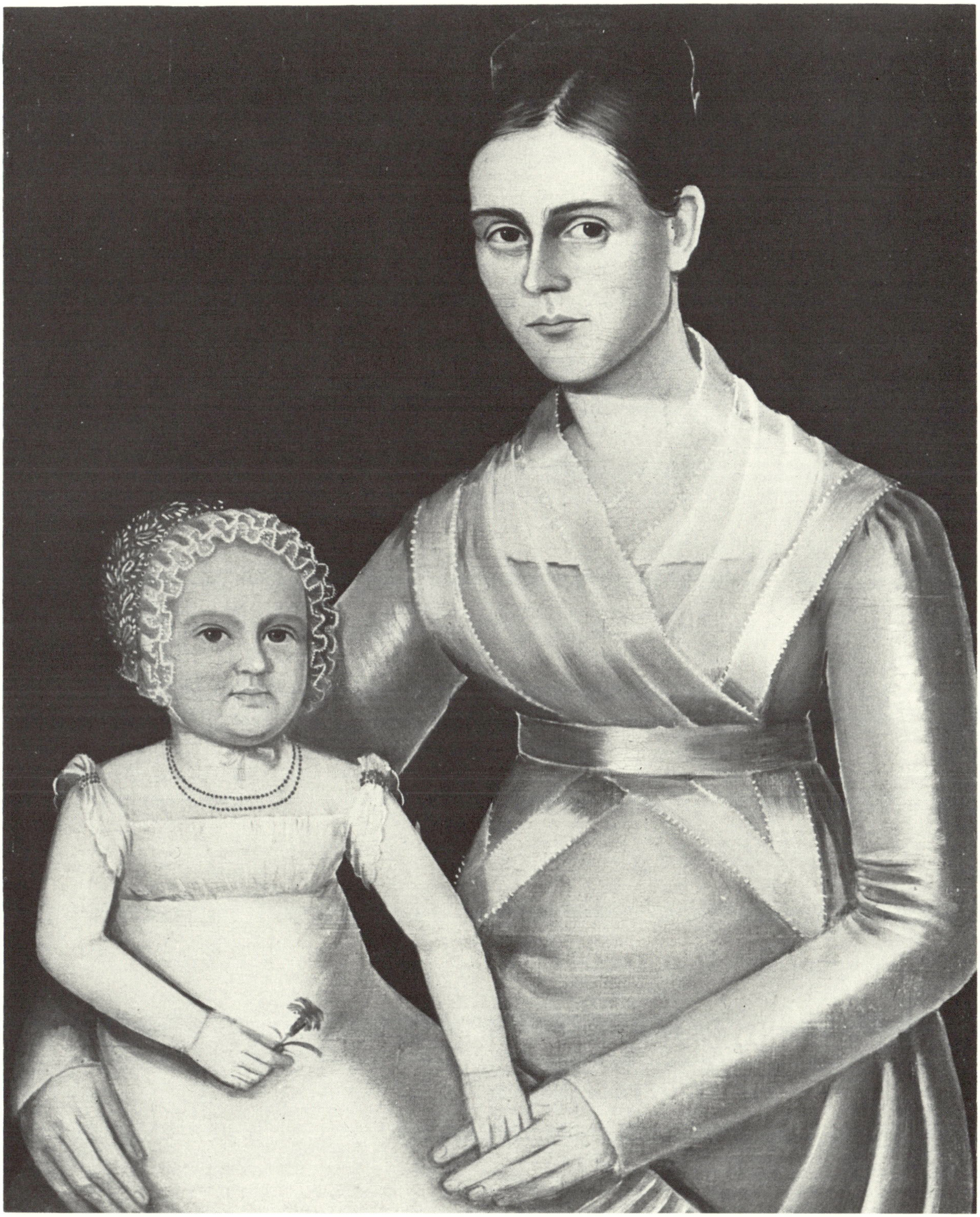

Mother and Child in White. *Oil by Ammi Phillips, ca. 1820.*

Adam and Eve. *Wood carving by Edgar Tolson, 1970.*

Dancing Negro. *Detail of a trade sign, artist unknown, about 1850.*

Folk Art, including the painting, One Shoe Off, *by John Brewster.*

The Farmers' Museum

Across Route 80 from Fenimore House lies The Farmers' Museum—first, the impressive stone barn which Mr. Stephen C. Clark, Sr. called "my brother's cow palace," then to the south the dozen or so buildings brought in from the surrounding area to suggest a crossroads village. As a sign at the entrance suggests, here is told "the story of how the plain people of yesterday, in doing their daily work built a great nation where only a great forest had stood." Indeed, how men and women worked, what tools and implements they used, process and product are the central themes of this pre-industrial museum, but attention is also paid to the amenities that make life bearable—religion, education, health and the home.

It has always been the desideratum at The Farmers' Museum that not only the tool but the hand that holds it, the handskill within the hand should make evident what is being explained. Sheer cost makes this impossible for every exhibit, but where feasible the human hand, using the ancient tool, makes clear what otherwise is so often difficult to understand.

One area in which to see this is in the textile exhibit where the dried flax is broken, scutched and hetchelled, transforming the stiff straws into handfuls of soft threads that bring to mind the word flaxen. Then the visitors gather around the flax wheel while a

Folk Art, including cigar store Indian by the slave Job, ca. 1810.

knowing hand feeds the strands to the spindle that twists it into thread; thence, to the loom where the dyed threads are woven into the pattern pre-established by the weaver. No pictures, no movie, no video can make this ancient metamorphosis as clear as can the patient worker who is able and willing to answer questions and repeat a process on request.

In the Lippitt Farmhouse, beyond the Crossroads Village, other women are baking gingerbread in the beehive oven, or performing that other magic which changes cream into butter. The distinguished scholar and historian of historical agencies, Walter Muir Whitehill, once wrote of the Lippitt House:

I must say a word about the extraordinary honesty and vividness of the Lippitt House restoration. There are many historic houses of the 18th and 19th centuries that have been made so handsome that their original owners. . . would never recognize them. This is part of a lamentable

Farmers' Museum. The Village Street: left to right, lawyer's office, druggist shop, doctor's office, print shop, blacksmith shop.

Farmers' Museum, main building.

tendency to prettify and idealize the past; to try to make it more elegant than it ever was in fact; to forget that the past, like the present was more often than not tasteless and grubby. Had the Lippitt House fallen into the hands of tasteful persons with romantic ideas its panelling would have been scraped and refinished, its sills repaired, its paint made spotless. . . . As it is, scrawny hens run about, the door frame is mangy, the cat hole remains available for use, the sofa in the best parlor is ragged; the whole place presents a scene of rural life that is, in my experience unmatched in its vividness and honesty.

Whitehill caught and verbalized a major tenet of those who brought The Farmers' Museum into being, but especially of Stephen Clark—to do ones best to show country life between the Revolution and the Civil War as honestly as possible, the past as it was, not as latter day nice Nellies might wish it to have been. And this was true not only of Lippitt House, but of every exhibit, every statement in the museum.

The fields nearby Lippitt House are plowed with the oxen from the pasture, appropriate crops are planted. A team of horses, a sow

Farmers' Museum. Bump Tavern. Opposite page: The Farmers' Museum church, with the lake beyond, and the schoolhouse and country store, with the blacksmith shop in the distance.

Lippitt farmhouse and barns.

and her litter, a wandering flocklet of sheep are about, while in the pond a new family of ducks paddle about, if they can escape the snapping turtle that lives there.

A small building houses a printer who turns out broadsides or up-to-date copies of the *Otsego Herald.* Once the building stood in Middlefield where it had, indeed, been a print shop. Carefully photographed, the stones were cleaned and numbered, the woodwork taken down and replaced only when it was unusable. When reconstructed and ready once again for its printing press, old neighbors of the building agreed that it looked as it always had looked.

This was the process with each of the buildings, first the school from Filer's Corners, then the country store from Toddsville and the smithy from New Berlin. After that the other buildings came on rapidly. The most complex was the Bump Tavern which was cut into twenty-one segments and then refitted together. While it was still in pieces, Nina Fletcher Little, the author of *Decorative American Wall Painting*, discovered that all the second floor walls had been stencilled and were in good enough condition to provide the colors and patterns adequate for restoration.

It took ten years to find the church waiting in Cornwallville not a dozen miles from Ashland where we had found the tavern. It had been moved twice before and once had had its face lifted, obscuring the earlier Gothic windows. But piece by piece it came to Cooperstown and was re-erected, beginning a new career housing musicals, sings, weddings and now and then a memorial service. The old organ from Cherry Valley is played a good deal and the church bell makes a lovely sound over the village street.

There is a saying about the men and women who painted the early portraits we call folk

Lippitt farmhouse kitchen.

Farmers' Museum activities. Above, relaxing between events at the Junior Livestock Show. Below: Harvest Festival, fiddlers on the porch at Bump Tavern. Braking flax in the main barn.

art, that they showed their sitters, "warts and all." There are always those who want to see the past as "the good old days." The fact is there never were any good old days. Dirt, flies, manure, unknown killing disease, death at childbirth for mother or babe, fear and weariness were the lot of our ancestors. No museum can emphasize those elements alone, nor should it, but it can make clear what was achieved despite these handicaps and that is what The Farmers' Museum does.

Since 1947 The Farmers' Museum has joined forces with the county 4-H to produce the annual Farmers' Museum Junior Livestock Show which has helped to upgrade the livestock raised by young farm folk in our area. In recent years the staff at Fenimore House and The Farmers' Museum have developed special occasions for the community to come and enjoy a harvest festival, or a Christmas sing, or earlier Christmas toys, or a gala spring opening day. These are devised to strengthen the bond between the village and the institutions, so that the village knows what is going on and can take pride in taking part. As the preceding pages make clear, this center for history is primarily concerned with interpreting the American past to our times and our citizens of all ages. It seeks to do it as honestly as possible, based on the best research and the best interpretation of which its staff is capable.

Bibliography

James Franklin Beard, editor: *Letters and Journals of James Fenimore Cooper,* 6 vols.; Cambridge, Mass., 1960–1968.

Ralph Birdsall: *The Story of Cooperstown,* Cooperstown, 1917.

Biographical Review of Otsego County, N.Y., New York, 1893.

Henry E. Boynton: *James Fenimore Cooper,* New York, 1931.

James Fenimore Cooper: *The Chronicles of Cooperstown* (1838), Cooperstown, 1929.

______*The Deerslayer, Or, The First Warpath,* 1841.

______*The Pioneers, Or, The Sources of the Susquehanna,* 1823.

James Fenimore Cooper [The Younger]: *The Legends and Traditions of a Northern County,* Cooperstown, 1936.

______*Reminiscences of Mid-Victorian Cooperstown and Sketch of William Cooper,* Cooperstown, 1936.

William Cooper: *A Guide in the Wilderness,* Dublin, 1810 [reprint, Cooperstown, 1936].

James Taylor Dunn: *Cardiff Giant Hoax,* Cooperstown, 1949.

[Alexander Flick]: *The American Revolution in New York*, Albany, 1926.

Francis Whiting Halsey: *The Old New York Frontier*, New York, 1901 [reprint, Port Washington, N.Y., 1963].

Charles Henry Hart: *Browere's Life Masks of Great Americans*, Philadelphia, 1898.

Robert W. Henderson: *Ball, Bat and Bishop,* New York, 1947.

Harold H. Hollis: *History of Cooperstown,* Cooperstown, 1976.

Ken Smith: *Baseball's Hall of Fame,* New York, 1947.

Richard Smith: *A Tour of Four Great Rivers,* edited by Francis Whiting Halsey, New York, 1906.

A.G. Spalding: *America's National Game,* New York, 1911.

Robert E. Spiller: *Fenimore Cooper, Critic of His Times*, New York, 1931.

Glyndon G. Van Deusen: *Thurlow Weed, Wizard of the Lobby,* Boston, 1947.

Albert Tangeman Volwiler: *George Croghan and the Westward Movement, 1741–1782,* Cleveland, 1926.

Paintings, art objects and photographs are in the following collections of the New York State Historical Association: Fenimore House collections, pp. 13, 14, 23, 24, 25, 27, 45, 86, 87, 88, 89, 90, 92, 93, 94, 95, 96, 97, 100, 102, 103. Library Special Collections, p. 22. Smith-Telfer Collection, pp. 32, 39, 43 bottom, 44, 52, 53. Ward Collection, pp. 39 top, 56.

Credit for photographs: Mary Imogene Bassett Hospital, pp. 72, 73, 75, 78, 79, 80, 81. Emmet Blum, *Oneonta Star,* p. 62. Cooperstown *Freeman's Journal,* pp. 54, 55. Ron Domin, p. 84 top. National Baseball Hall of Fame and Museum, pp. 49, 58, 61, 65, 66, 68, 69. Gerard Reese, p. 104 top. G.E. Kidder Smith, pp. 16, 29, 34, 38, 40, 41, 42, 43 top, 51, 60, 76, 85, 98, 99, 101 bottom, Milo V. Stewart, pp. 18, 19, 46, 84 bottom, 95, 100, 101 top, 104 bottom left. Dante Tranquille, p. 104 bottom right. Wurts Brothers, pp. 10, 17, 36, 50. Mark Zeek, p. 57

Cover photo: Milo V. Stewart.